OUTRAGEOUS
ANIMAL
ADAPTATIONS

FROM **BIG-EARED BATS**
TO **FRILL-NECKED LIZARDS**

MICHAEL J. ROSEN

TWENTY-FIRST CENTURY BOOKS / MINNEAPOLIS

*The author would like to express his gratitude to
Christoffer Strömstedt for help during the initial research
and drafting of entries for an earlier version of this book.*

Twenty-First Century Books
A division of Lerner Publishing Group, Inc.
241 First Avenue North
Minneapolis, MN 55401 USA

For reading levels and more information, look up this title at www.lernerbooks.com.

Main body text set in Avenir LT Pro 11/15.
Typeface provided by Adobe Systems.

Library of Congress Cataloging-in-Publication Data

The Cataloging-in-Publication Data for *Outrageous Animal Adaptations:
From Big-Eared Bats to Frill-Necked Lizards* is on file at the Library of Congress.
ISBN 978-1-5124-2999-2 (lib. bdg.)
ISBN 978-1-5124-9885-1 (EB pdf)

Manufactured in the United States of America
1-41601-23506-9/8/2017

TABLE OF CONTENTS

The proboscis monkey has evolved a large nose that amplifies its calls to warn other monkeys of danger. These monkeys also swim to avoid predators.

INTRODUCTION
EVOLUTIONARY ELEGANCE

When I was young, my parents enrolled me in a book club about nature. Each month a volume about an ecosystem or grouping of related animal species appeared in our mailbox. Most pages in each of the paperback volumes featured an empty box that readers were invited to fill with a photo of the correct animal. The volumes provided the photos in a grouping of separate pages of full-color photographs. It was my job to place each of the photographs in the correct empty box in the book's pages.

I acquired book after book—*Life in the Everglades, Wildlife of Australia, Birds of Prey.* I felt as if I were traveling the world, adding creature after creature to my list, as if I had encountered them on safaris and expeditions.

EXPLORING NATURE

I spent much of my childhood with this zeal for the natural world. Yet it might have been my ninth-grade honors biology class that ignited my passion to be a naturalist. There, I peered through microscopes at my own eyelashes and then, adjusting the lens, at insect scales and skin cells. I handled tarantulas and hummingbirds encased in Plexiglas cubes and glass tubes. I listened to tapes of howler monkeys and whale songs. I puzzled my way through the taxonomic naming system that organizes the whole of the plant and animal kingdoms, memorizing each species, genus, family, order, class, and phylum. But most profoundly, these experiences created an unquenchable curiosity. They convinced me how tiny our human presence is when compared to the planet's nearly immeasurable diversity.

EXTREME ELEGANCE

As an adult, I live on a 100-acre (40.5 ha) farm in the foothills of the Appalachian Mountains. I continually see how every creature, in its own competitive niche, has evolved ways to compete for territory and mates, and to eat and not be eaten.

Michael J. Rosen and his Australian Stumpy Tail Cattle Dog live and explore in the Ohio foothills of the Appalachians.

This book showcases animals whose survival strategies are among the planet's most extreme. Every creature in the book proves how elegantly, over thousands of generations, a species can transform—in size, shape, color, behavior, or sensory abilities—to meet the challenges necessary to survive and ensure the future of its kind. In fields such as biology, chemistry, and math, the word *elegant* hardly means "chic" or "smartly dressed." Rather, elegance refers to simplicity, concision, and a concept's ability to truly solve the problem it addresses. For example, when the nineteenth-century English biologist Thomas Henry Huxley read about Charles Darwin's theory of evolution and natural

Charles Darwin publicly introduced his theory of evolution in 1858. The theory states that all of life is related. Complex creatures evolve from simple organisms over time through genetic mutation. The mutations that help organisms survive are preserved and passed to the next generation.

selection, he reportedly commented, "How extremely stupid not to have thought of that!"

The axolotl's mane of frilly gills and the naked mole rat's squinty, buck-toothed face and the proboscis monkey's reddish honker may seem bizarre or outrageous. But each represents something simultaneously simple and yet decisive. Each feature or adaptation solves a particular predicament in a purposeful manner.

So even if you gasp or cringe—or even furrow your brow in disgust—as you read about the two dozen oddities featured here, I hope you'll also marvel at their elegance—at the exquisite adaptations each remarkable survivor has evolved.

TOWNSEND'S BIG-EARED BAT
LIFE (ALMOST) WITHOUT GRAVITY
(Corynorhinus townsendii)

Sure, you say, bats have some amazing traits. For example, the tube-lipped nectar bat's tongue is one and a half times longer than its entire body. It's so long it retracts all the way into its rib cage—and may take the prize for the battiest body part. But the length of the ears of the Townsend's big-eared bat, at 1.5 inches (3.8 cm), is one-third of this little critter's body length. And far from clumsy, these pinnae, or outer ears, are surprisingly useful.

During an evening hunt, this insectivore (insect eater) is all ears. The pinnae can extend completely forward or lay back along the bat's body. Using echolocation, the bat tracks its prey. When sound waves bounce off a moth or other tasty morsel, the bat's satellite-dish ears pick up the sounds again. Then the bat's brain can pinpoint the prey's size and course of flight by comparing the information that each ear gathers. For instance, a louder echo bounce back means a larger insect is reflecting the sound. If the left ear reports the echo first, that means make a left for the next bite!

When the bats aren't hunting, they're hanging. Hanging upside down offers a bat an advantage. Roosting in high places, they're out of reach from many predators. There's plenty of unoccupied real estate for hanging under a bridge or on the craggy ceiling of a cave too. To help the bat's inverted lifestyle, each foot has evolved a locking tendon to keep the bat's toes in a gripping position. When the bat is hanging upside down, its own weight causes its toes to close around whatever the bat's holding onto. The tendon locks into place so the bat can relax rather than continually contracting its muscles to hold tight.

The bat's big ears are useful here too. During hibernation, the bat hangs out (literally) in a roosting place called a hibernaculum. Its ears curl up—looking oddly similar to the horns of a bighorn sheep—to help regulate the bat's body temperature. Folded in, the blood

ADAPTATIONS

This bat uses its huge ears for echolocation. The bat makes a series of high-pitched sounds and listens for the sounds to bounce back from the environment. This allows the bat to figure out where things are. The ears also help the bat lift off into flight and regulate its body temperature.

CLASSIFICATION

Kingdom: Animalia (animals)
Phylum: Chordata (chordates, or animals with a flexible rod of cells to support the body)
Subphylum: Vertebrata (true vertebrates, or animals with spinal cords)
Class: Mammalia (mammals)
Order: Chiroptera (bats)
Suborder: Microchiroptera (micro-, or small, bats)
Family: Vespertilionidae (evening bats or common bats)
Genus: *Corynorhinus* (big-eared bats)
Species: *C. townsendii* (Townsend's big-eared bat)

Distribution: western North America, from Canada to southern Mexico
Conservation status: Least Concern

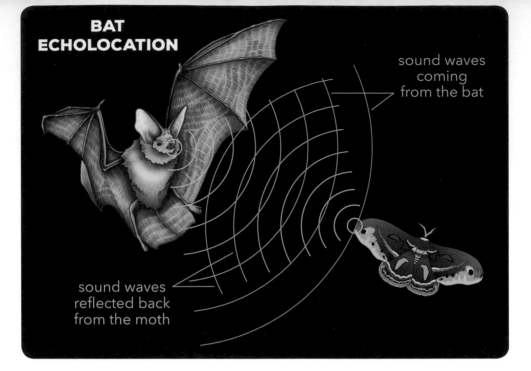

BAT ECHOLOCATION

sound waves coming from the bat

sound waves reflected back from the moth

vessels in the thin skin of the ears hold onto heat. Unfurled, they release heat.

Unlike flying squirrels that float briefly and humans that fall quickly through the air, bats are the one mammal that can truly fly. But bat wings aren't strong enough to provide lift from a standing position. And the rear legs aren't strong enough to generate lift from a running start. So the bat's huge ears, like the wings of an airplane, provide a bit of lift during takeoffs and landings. How does a bat take off? It lets go of whatever it's hanging onto, and the wings take over!

CURIOUS FACT

Heavyweights such as humans immediately feel gravity's pull on our blood when we simply bend over. Imagine if we tried to hang from our ankles on a jungle gym for any amount of time! Talk about dizzy! By contrast, even the heaviest of the nine hundred to twelve hundred bat species that occupy the planet weighs no more than 2.5 pounds (1 kg). Bats are such lightweights that gravity's steady pull doesn't increase pressure in their heads and blood vessels when they hang upside down.

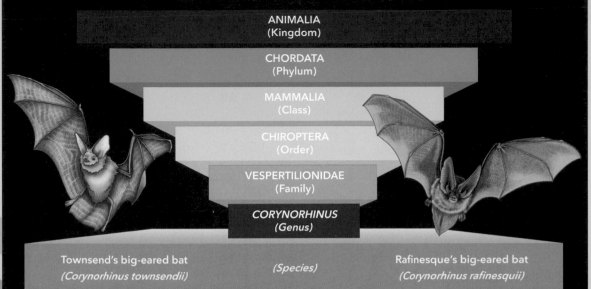

BIG-EARED BAT TAXONOMY

ANIMALIA
(Kingdom)

CHORDATA
(Phylum)

MAMMALIA
(Class)

CHIROPTERA
(Order)

VESPERTILIONIDAE
(Family)

CORYNORHINUS
(Genus)

Townsend's big-eared bat
(Corynorhinus townsendii)

(Species)

Rafinesque's big-eared bat
(Corynorhinus rafinesquii)

ABOUT TAXONOMY

Taxonomy is the system of naming, describing, and arranging species into specific classifications. These divisions, as well as the names of groups and species, continually evolve as new creatures are discovered and as research techniques develop. For example, the bobbit worm's original description and naming was based on a single specimen collected in Sri Lanka in 1788. Over time, people documented more sea worm specimens in a variety of other locations. They noticed differences in size, shape, and color, so the sea worm's classification was overhauled repeatedly as more information was gathered.

Taxonomy enjoys—*endures* might be more accurate—ongoing revisions. The taxonomy in this book reflects the most accepted nomenclature (naming) and classification at the time of writing. Even during the final months of this book's production, a new species of Galápagos giant tortoise was announced. Michel Milinkovitch of Switzerland's University of Geneva and a Galápagos tortoise specialist said of the new species, "Call them whatever you want, I don't care. What is important is that people realize there is hidden diversity [in the natural world]." What is hiding in plain sight is what the difficult work of taxonomy continues to uncover.

C. townsendii and *C. rafinesqii* were once part of the genus *Plecotus*. Scientists later determined that *Corynorhinus* was a distinct genus.

Aye-ayes are recognizable by their long, bony fingers. They also have large eyes and ears and a bushy tail that is larger than their body.

AYE-AYE
DRUMMING UP FOOD

(Daubentonia madagascariensis)

Canadian drummer Tom Grosset holds the current record in Extreme Sport Drumming. His drumsticks can tick off 1,208 strokes in a minute. That's just over 20 per second. Impressively, the planet's largest nocturnal primate, the aye-aye, approaches that record with just one finger when it's hungry. It can tap eight times per second. Go ahead, try it. Bet you can't tap your fingers eight times in a second!

The aye-aye lives in Madagascar, an island nation off the southeastern coast of Africa. It is an insect-eating mammal—a warm-blooded, hair-covered vertebrate. Like other mammals, mother aye-ayes feed their milk to their live-born young. And aye-ayes have only one predator: the fossa (*Cryptoprocta ferox*), a large, catlike mammal. With so few enemies, the aye-aye is able to live in a wide variety of habitats in Madagascar. Most impressively, the aye-aye knows percussion! It's the only primate that uses echolocation, which it uses to forage for food. Instead of hammering into branches and logs with a beak, the way a woodpecker does, the aye-aye taps its fingers like drumsticks on the woody surfaces. Then the aye-aye's comically large, movable, funnel-shaped ears listen carefully. If the returning echoes suggest ants, larvae, or other tunneling insects, the aye-aye's rodent-like teeth gnaw a hole into the wood. The aye-aye slips its skeletal and flexible middle finger—the tip can curl forward and backward—inside the hole to snatch up the snack and bring it back to its mouth. The aye-aye also eats coconut meat, fruits, nuts, and nectar. These meals don't require echolocation,

ADAPTATIONS

The aye-aye is the largest of all nocturnal primates (apes that are active mostly at night). It has also evolved some interesting meal-seeking methods. It is the only primate to find food using echolocation, and it has an exceptionally long and flexible middle finger for finding and snatching up food.

CLASSIFICATION

Kingdom: Animalia (animals)
Phylum: Chordata (chordates, or animals with a flexible rod of cells to support the body)
Subphylum: Vertebrata (true vertebrates)
Class: Mammalia (mammals)
Order: Primates (primates)
Family: Daubentoniidae (aye-ayes)
Genus: *Daubentonia* (two species of aye-aye, with one extinct)
Species: *D. madagascariensis* (Madagascar aye-aye)

Like rodents, aye-ayes have long incisors (narrow teeth at the front of the mouth, used for cutting). These teeth are always growing. In fact, until 1850, scientists thought the aye-aye was a rodent. Later, after close examination of the aye-aye's skeleton, body shape, and posture, scientists decided the aye-aye fit better among lemurs, another animal unique to Madagascar. Lemurs are a group of mostly nocturnal primates that have long noses and walk on all fours, rather than upright as many other primates do.

Distribution: Madagascar
Conservation status: Endangered

but the animal still spends 80 percent of every night drumming up grub. This percussive foraging is one of nature's most tedious drum solos . . . and probably boring enough for the rest of us to snooze through.

An aye-aye sticks its long middle finger into a branch to scoop out its food.

Opposable thumbs and sticky pads on the fingers and toes help this tree frog move through the tree branches of its home.

WAXY MONKEY TREE FROG
(Phyllomedusa sauvagii)

THE FROG THAT USES SUNSCREEN

CLASSIFICATION

Kingdom: Animalia (animals)

Phylum: Chordata (chordates, or animals with a flexible rod of cells to support the body)

Class: Amphibia (amphibians including frogs and salamanders)

Order: Anura (frogs)

Family: Hylidae (hylids, frogs that live in trees)

Subfamily: Phyllomedusinae (South and Central American tree frogs)

Genus: *Phyllomedusa* (frogs that deposit their eggs on leaves)

Species: *P. sauvagii* (waxy monkey tree frog or painted monkey frog)

Distribution: warm, dry forests throughout central South America

Conservation status: Least Concern

Herpetologists (those who study reptiles and amphibians) seem to enjoy giving colorful common names to freaky frogs. The Pac-Man frog, Pinocchio frog, and hip-pocket frog are three real examples. The waxy monkey tree frog, also known as the painted-belly leaf frog for the splotchy patterns on its underside, is no exception. In the extreme heat of its South American habitat, much of this tree frog's survival depends on saving water. One way it does this is by producing a waxy substance that it spreads over its skin with its legs. It's like applying sunscreen, but it's to prevent water loss rather than sunburn. Thanks to that adaptation, these frogs are among the few amphibians that can tolerate direct sunlight. Even though they are ectotherms, or cold-blooded creatures—animals that take on the temperature of their environment—they can survive with a body temperature of up to 105.8°F (41°C), the highest of any amphibian. These tree frogs also save water by producing a semisolid, concentrated uric acid rather than watery urine. (Camels, which have similar water conservation techniques, expel a urine so concentrated that it's like a syrup—not that it would be good on pancakes.)

To stay cool during the hot daytime hours, these frogs exhibit what could be mistaken as a sleepy and bored posture. Called diurnal torpor, it's a calm, almost nonresponsive attitude. The frogs reserve the nighttime hours for activity, such as walking among the tree branches to feed on insects. To help with this nighttime activity, the frogs, like all tree frogs, have sticky pads on the fingers and toes for clinging and climbing. But this species also has opposable thumbs—one digit on each hand can touch the tips of that hand's other fingers. That's a talent shared only by pandas, koalas, opossums, and several primates—including humans. This earns the waxy monkey tree frog the distinction of being the one and only grasping frog—another zoological merit badge!

These frogs are hylids. They live their entire lives in the trees. During the rainy seasons, torrential rains create temporary ponds and lagoons in their habitat. The frogs build their leafy nests on a branch over these bodies of water. When the female frog is ready to spawn, or lay her eggs, she releases them on a leaf and then folds them inside the leaf to create an egg sandwich. When the eggs hatch, the tadpoles go for their first splash in the water below. Soon after, they sprout legs, swap their underwater breathing apparatus (gills) for above-water lungs, and bid their watery nursery goodbye forever. Once they're able, each climbs a nearby tree and calls it home for the eight or so years of its life.

The mudskipper's eyes are on top of its head so it can raise its eyes to see above the water.

MUDSKIPPER
A LIFE ON LAND AND SEA

(Periophthalmus magnuspinnatus)

A flying bird that takes a plunge into the water—perfectly natural, right? But a swimming fish that takes to the trees? Say hello to the planet's most athletic fish. Known as kangaroo fish, mudhoppers, or johnny jumpers, mudskippers grow to be about 3.7 inches (9.5 cm) long. They have fins, gills, and a long tail. Some leave the water only at low tide (when the water pulls back from the shore). Some live on mud flats (muddy lands exposed only during low tide). And others spend more time outside of the water than in it.

Fish use organs called gills to get oxygen from water. Most amphibians breathe through lungs and by absorbing oxygen through their skin. Mudskippers breathe with gills, but they can also breathe through their skin like an amphibian, as long as the skin stays moist. This is called cutaneous respiration. To further help these fish breathe out of water, they store pockets of water around their gills. The water keeps the gills wet so they will continue to take in oxygen, even when the mudskipper is on land.

To further assist its double life, the mudskipper's eyeballs are more like those of a frog or an alligator than a fish—they're plopped right on top of the head like bubbles rather than placed to the sides. So the mudskipper can raise its eyes above the water. After a few minutes of scoping things out, the mudskipper can pull its eyeballs back into its head for a quick rinse and then pop them back out again.

In water the mudskipper's front fins can spread like wings. And with a few beats of its long tail, the mudskipper can glide just under the surface, getting lift from the fins so it doesn't sink low in the water. On land it can walk on those fins in a movement that ichthyologists (fish scientists) call crutching. And it does look a lot like a person moving on crutches: the

ADAPTATIONS

This amphibious fish can breathe air, walk on land, climb trees, and leap up to 2 feet (60 cm) into the air. And its bulging eyes can see above and below water at the same time—that's double the vantage points, a clear advantage.

CLASSIFICATION

Kingdom: Animalia (animals)
Phylum: Chordata (chordates, or animals with a flexible rod of cells to support the body)
Subphylum: Vertebrata (true vertebrates)
Class: Actinopterygii (ray-finned fishes, fish with fins supported by bony spines)
Order: Perciformes (perch-like fishes, including perch, bass, and bluegill)
Family: Gobiidae (small, carnivorous fish such as gobies)
Subfamily: Oxudercinae (mudskippers)
Genus: *Periophthalmus* (mudskippers whose eyes, like periscopes, can look around)
Species: *P. magnuspinnatus* (big-finned mudskipper)

Distribution: coastal areas of the Pacific and Indian Oceans
Conservation status: Not Evaluated

mudskipper's front fins reach forward, pull the body forward, and then stretch ahead again for another step.

The mudskipper can stand upright on its tail fins too. These tiny acrobats can also catapult into the air—leaping, flipping, and performing tail springs.

A NOTE ON EVOLUTIONARY TIME

Animal adaptation is fluid, ongoing, and essential for survival. But it can be difficult to imagine how these changes occur. Changes develop over thousands or millions of years among countless species with millions of genes. Most scientists agree that evolution happens naturally, step by step over time. Evolutionary biologists say that nearly 350 to 400 million years ago, fish evolved into the planet's first land animals. This evolution involved adaptations to nearly every bone, organ, sense, and behavior.

To explore further how fish could have evolved into land animals, a team of biologists at Canada's McGill University raised two groups of bichir fish. These fish have a body shape similar to early tetrapods. They can breathe air and are able to use their fins to propel themselves forward on land. The research team raised one group of fish in water. They raised the other group in tanks that mimicked land-based life, with very shallow water only. They misted the fish continually so they would not dry out. The

This mudskipper's fins are extended beneath it, helping it move through the mud.

team wanted to see if the fish in the shallow-water tanks might eventually develop morphology (body shape) that would allow them to walk more easily.

In 2014 the team published their results. They found that within eight months, the bones and muscles of the shallow-water-raised fish were already showing changes. A neck between the head and body seemed to be developing, and bones in the chest and shoulders changed so the fish could support more weight on their fins. The fish planted their fins closer to their bodies to support themselves while moving on land and could lift their heads higher off the ground to move forward more easily. This experiment shows how fish may have adapted as they moved from water to land millions of years ago. The team believes the research begins to show how quickly and easily creatures adapt to new environments. Over time, through changes such as the ones found in the experiment, fish evolved into the millions of land creatures that inhabit Earth.

CURIOUS FACT

All life began in the world's oceans. Over time, some animals left the water to live on land. They evolved various traits and organs to survive there. For example, they adapted their fins to walk on land, and their gills evolved to breathe in air. Aquatic life-forms also had to find a new way to swallow. In water a sucking action works to draw in a meal along with the surrounding water. But in air on land, this sucking doesn't work the same way. So about 350 to 400 million years ago, a line of four-legged land dwellers known as tetrapods evolved a tongue to help with food intake.

The mudskipper doesn't have a tongue, though, so it has a different strategy. It spits out water that it carries in its mouth. Food such as shrimp gets caught in the water—much like a frog's fleshy tongue might dart forward to grab a fly. Then the mudskipper sucks the water and food back inside its mouth. The mudskipper inhales each bite in less than half a second. "This could be an in-between [evolutionary stage], from which a fleshy tongue could have evolved," says Krijn Michel, a researcher at Belgium's University of Antwerp.

In the wild, axolotls are typically brown or black. White axolotls have become common among axolotls bred in captivity.

AXOLOTL
LIFE AS A JUVENILE

(Ambystoma mexicanum)

Imagine if a tadpole grew its legs, gills, and tail, and then, like Peter Pan, declared that it would never-never grow up into a frog. That's the general idea at work with the axolotl. This animal is a type of salamander that keeps physical characteristics from its young life even as a mature adult. In the axolotl's case, its tadpole-like form—the larval, or immature, body that lives in water—becomes an adult. Unlike other amphibians, it never emerges onto land or loses its baby face the way other mature salamanders do. The axolotl develops well beyond the size of a typical larval salamander, and yet it achieves sexual maturity (the ability to reproduce) even with juvenile characteristics. So the axolotl is part kid, part adult.

Many adult amphibians use cutaneous respiration—they breathe through the skin rather than through an organ such as gills or lungs. But axolotls have developed a funky hybrid form of breathing. They breathe using their skin, gills, *and* lungs. Check out those frilly branches that frame the axolotl's unblinking eyes and thick neck. They may look like a lion's mane, but they are actually external gills. The fancy fringe, known as rami, provides more surface area so the axolotl can take in more oxygen from the water. It only has to come to the surface occasionally to gulp air into its primitive lungs.

Unlike an axolotl, an adult salamander no longer has gills. Its limbs are more muscular, and its skin is thicker. These changes help the salamander live on land.

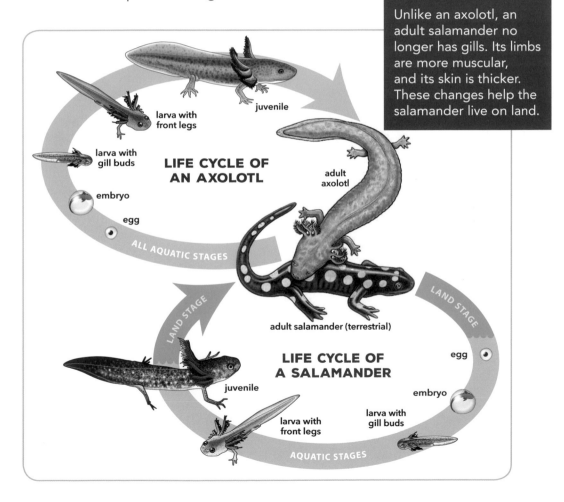

LIFE CYCLE OF AN AXOLOTL

larva with front legs

juvenile

larva with gill buds

embryo

egg

ALL AQUATIC STAGES

adult axolotl

adult salamander (terrestrial)

LAND STAGE

LAND STAGE

LIFE CYCLE OF A SALAMANDER

juvenile

larva with front legs

larva with gill buds

embryo

egg

AQUATIC STAGES

ADAPTATIONS

This species retains much of its juvenile body form throughout its entire life, even as an adult. This is called neoteny. Axolotls also have an exceptional ability to regenerate body parts.

CLASSIFICATION

Kingdom: Animalia (animals)
Phylum: Chordata (chordates, or animals with a flexible rod of cells to support the body)
Subphylum: Vertebrata (true vertebrates)
Class: Amphibia (frogs, salamanders, and other amphibians)
Family: Ambystomatidae (mole salamanders, salamanders that live in North America and Mexico)
Genus: *Ambystoma* (mole salamanders)
Species: *A. mexicanum* (Mexican salamander, or axolotl)

Distribution: freshwater lakes around Mexico City, many of which are being drained as the city expands
Conservation status: Critically Endangered

Axolotls range in size from 6 to 18 inches (15 to 45 cm), though they are most often around 9 inches (23 cm) long. Their skin colors vary from brown with spots to black.

In true sci-fi fashion, axolotls have fantastic regenerative powers. They can regrow most body parts. And they can heal their own wounds—*not* with scar tissue, the way most animals heal—but by growing completely new tissue. Along with this superpower, the body cells of an axolotl are unusually large, and their unhatched offspring are easy to keep alive. So lab researchers use axolotls to study genetics, the brain and nervous system, and how creatures grow.

It can't be long until we see a human-size axolotl as the avenging mutant-superhero in a new comic-book-inspired movie. Maybe, for ease of pronunciation, it will be known as the Ax.

THE DOUBLE LIFE OF AMPHIBIANS

Amphibians bridge the aquatic lifestyle of fish and the terrestrial (land-based) life of some reptiles. In fact, the word *amphibian* comes from the Greek words *amphi*, for "both," and *bios*, for "life."

All amphibians begin life in springtime when the water begins to warm. A female spawns her eggs in a jellylike string or bubble. The male deposits sperm on the eggs to fertilize them. After the embryo develops for a week or more, a tadpole—the amphibian's juvenile, or larval, form—will hatch. A tadpole's external gills draw oxygen for breathing from the water. It feeds on plant matter or plankton. A tail helps the tadpole move through the water.

As tadpoles grow in size, they begin to go through the transformations necessary for an adult life on land. Their gills move inside their bodies and eventually disappear as internal lungs begin to develop. Four legs begin to emerge. (In frogs and toads, the tail eventually disappears.) The tadpoles also change from vegetarians to meat eaters. Typically, these transformations take about four or five months. But most amphibians do not fully reach adulthood until they are three or four years old. Each winter, the young amphibians hibernate and continue to develop in the spring. Once the amphibians reach adulthood, the life cycle begins again in the water when a female spawns and a male fertilizes the eggs.

While geoducks burrow deep into the sand with their foot, the siphon sticks up out of the sand into the water so the geoduck can feed on plankton.

GEODUCK
A LIFE (ALMOST) WITHOUT AGING
(Panopea generosa)

Pronounced "gooey duck," the world's largest burrowing clam is neither gooey—*yuck!*—nor even remotely ducky. Its name is thought to come from a word meaning "dig deep" in the language of the Nisqualli, an American Indian nation near Washington's Puget Sound. The clam is also known as the elephant trunk clam, but that's really not much better. What elephant wants to settle down with a sand-packed snoot?

These huge clams tip the scales at an average of 3 pounds (1.4 kg), but some get much heavier than that. And their shells can span 6 to 8 inches (15 to 20 cm). So far, so big. But it's the siphon, or neck, that's really gargantuan. It can stretch more than 3 feet (1 m) long. In some extreme cases, the clam's siphon has grown to 6.5 feet (2 m) long—the length of an adult elephant's trunk.

Like many other clams, geoducks use their siphon to suck in water and plankton through a hole known as the inhalant channel. After the plankton settles out, the geoduck shoots out the strained water through a second hole, the exhalant channel. This process of sorting out the plankton from water is known as filter feeding.

To escape predators, the geoduck can retract into its shell. It pulls back its neck by shooting out a jet of water through both the inhalant and exhalant channels of its siphon.

Among the planet's true senior citizens, geoducks can live for as long as 160 years! (Few people bother to remember clams' birthdays anymore or send them cards.) The animals use their powerful ax-shaped foot to burrow under the sand of a tidal shore, where they anchor themselves for life.

ADAPTATION

These clams can live a century and a half, burrowed underneath the ocean sand where few predators will find them. Living on a diet of plankton (tiny living things that float in Earth's oceans) that whole time, they can grow to weigh as much as 16 pounds (7.3 kg).

CLASSIFICATION

Kingdom: Animalia (animals)
Phylum: Mollusca (mollusks, or marine invertebrates such as snails, squids, and clams)
Class: Bivalvia (bivalves, or animals with two-hinged shell parts such as oysters and clams)
Order: Myoida (marine clams including softshells, shipworms, and geoducks)
Family: Hiatellidae (rock-boring clams)
Genus: *Panopea* (geoducks)
Species: *P. generosa* (geoduck, also known as elephant-trunk clam, mud duck, or king clam)

Distribution: the western Pacific Ocean shores of North America
Conservation status: Not Evaluated

CURIOUS FACT

Clams have growth rings on the outside of their shells. The number of rings indicates the clam's age. Scientists typically count the rings inside a clam's hinge as these rings are protected and more likely to be accurate.

British scientists found a quahog clam in Iceland in 2006 that was 507 years old. The rings inside the clam's hinge were compressed into a small area and were difficult to count. So to determine its age, they used carbon 14 dating. This process measures the amount of radiocarbon in a specimen. Radiocarbon occurs naturally in plants and animals and decays at a known rate. So when an organism dies, scientists measure the amount of radiocarbon in the organism to figure out the animal's age at death.

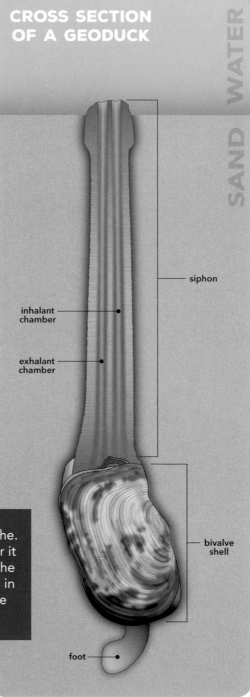

CROSS SECTION OF A GEODUCK

WATER

SAND

siphon

inhalant chamber

exhalant chamber

bivalve shell

foot

A geoduck uses its siphon to eat and breathe. It pulls plankton and oxygen from the water it sucks in through the inhalant chamber. As the geoduck grows, its foot becomes too small in relation to its body to dig any farther, so the clam stays put for years.

Giant cuttlefish have eight arms and two longer tentacles. The fin along the length of the body helps the cuttlefish move smoothly in the water.

GIANT CUTTLEFISH
LIVING SUBMARINES

(Sepia apama)

Giant cuttlefish are highly intelligent, brilliantly colored, and have what looks like an incredibly impressive moustache. (That moustache is actually the cuttlefish's eight arms and two long tentacles that it uses for eating, mating, and camouflage.) They're basically living submarines—OK, submarines with a bit of an odd shape. Cuttlefish weigh as much as 23 pounds (11 kg) and are related to mollusks such as snails and lobsters. But unlike those mollusks, the cuttlefish doesn't have a shell—or does it? The shell

ADAPTATIONS

The giant cuttlefish has a cuttlebone to stay afloat and to sink. It has W-shaped pupils in its exceptionally well-developed eyes and incredible camouflage skills.

CLASSIFICATION

Kingdom: Animalia (animals)
Phylum: Mollusca (invertebrates including snails, squid, clams, and relatives)
Class: Cephalopoda (cephalopods such as octopuses, squid, and cuttlefish)
Order: Sepiida (cuttlefish)
Family: Sepiidae (cuttlefish)
Genus: *Sepia* (cuttlefish)
Species: *S. apama* (Australian giant cuttlefish)

Distribution: the southern coast of Australia, Indian Ocean, and islands in the southwestern Pacific Ocean
Conservation status: Near Threatened

is actually inside the cuttlefish's body and is called a cuttlebone. This hollow structure holds gas and liquid and helps the creature to rise and sink in water. Like a submarine, the giant cuttlefish rises and falls in the water by changing the amount of ballast, or the gas and liquid, that it holds in its body. This manipulation of ballast requires very little energy, so the cuttlefish can devote most of its energy to growing larger.

With the largest brain compared to body size of any invertebrate, a cuttlefish is a contender for undersea valedictorian. In scientific studies, cuttlefish have shown an ability to communicate and to learn by taking in information about their surroundings and making decisions about how to behave in the environment. For example, some cuttlefish were able to find their way through a maze. And cuttlefish eyes, with their unique W-shaped pupils, are among the most developed of any creature in the animal kingdom. Even unborn cuttlefish can see while still inside the partially see-through egg. Giant cuttlefish can see well in dim light, and although they are color-blind, they can perceive contrast. To focus, the cuttlefish changes the shape of its eyes, and the large size of the eyes may allow for greater magnification of images. Scientists believe the W-shape helps control how much light enters the eyes.

Giant cuttlefish can change their appearance in less than a second to better blend in with their surroundings.

If it's being stalked, the cuttlefish can squirt a brown pigment from its siphon, disappearing into a cloud of this ink. But it also has another amazing defense mechanism. This chameleon of the sea has skin covered with several types of specialized cells that allow it to change its color, texture, and pattern at will.

CURIOUS FACT

The giant cuttlefish might qualify as one of the planet's laziest creatures. The amount of energy it takes in as food compared to the energy it uses suggests that this creature has a sedentary, or inactive, lifestyle. It isn't really lazy, though. Its form of predation is to hide and wait for a meal to arrive rather than to burn calories searching for and chasing after prey.

To track the cuttlefish's motion, scientists used radio-acoustic positioning and telemetry (RAPT) to tag individual cuttlefish in Boston Bay, off South Australia, with tiny transmitters. These transmitters monitor changes in the patterns of waves as the cuttlefish move through water. They send information about this motion to nearby buoys equipped with hydrophones (microphones that receive sound waves in water). The data showed that 95 percent of the time, a giant squid is not moving much at all.

Colored cells known as chromatophores are arranged in a layer on its skin. Mostly black, brown, yellow, and red, these cells can individually blend to make different colors that match the cuttlefish's surroundings in a fraction of a second. Cells called iridophores provide additional flashes of light and color to enhance the camouflage. At the same time, a layer of cells called leucophores can change the creature's brightness. The cuttlefish can turn luminously bright or instantly dull, to disappear by matching the light—or lack of light—in its environment.

Using its circular muscles, the giant cuttlefish can also control papillae, or tiny bumps on the skin. This allows the texture and outline of the skin to blend into the seaweed, coral, or rock around the animal. These camouflage cells allow the cuttlefish to change colors quickly to hide, warn other cuttlefish, woo a mate, or ambush prey. Small male cuttlefish can even partially disguise themselves as females to sneak past beefier males. They display typically female patterns on one side of their bodies and their regular male pattern on the side facing the female. This tricks other males and allows the cuttlefish to woo the female without competition.

WEST INDIAN MANATEE
THE OCEAN'S ONE VEGETARIAN MAMMAL
(Trichechus manatus)

West Indian manatees spend between five and eight hours each day eating. They use their lips and flippers to dig up and grab food.

One glimpse of its lippy, bristly muzzle and you'll understand this massive sea mammal's nickname: sea cow. Manatees evolved from creatures that waded the sea-grass smorgasbord of shallow ocean waters about fifty million years ago. Daryl Domning, a professor of anatomy at Harvard University, suggests that its ancestor "probably looked something like an otter crossed with a hippopotamus." In modern times, a manatee typically weighs 1,000 pounds (454 kg) and is 10 feet (3 m) long. Some manatees

ADAPTATION
This slow-moving creature is the only marine mammal that lives on a plants-only diet.

CLASSIFICATION
Kingdom: Animalia (animals)
Phylum: Chordata (chordates, or animals with a flexible rod of cells to support the body)
Subphylum: Vertebrata (true vertebrates)
Class: Mammalia (mammals)
Order: Sirenia (three species of manatees as well as the dugong)
Family: Trichechidae (manatees)
Genus: *Trichechus* (manatees)
Species: *T. manatus* (West Indian manatee)

Distribution: Florida, northwestern Atlantic Ocean, and the Caribbean
Conservation status: Vulnerable

can exceed 3,300 pounds (1,497 kg) and 15 feet (5 m)!

Manatees have a unique history. Like all life on Earth, they evolved from the sea. They and other sea creatures eventually moved to land, where some evolved into mammals. Independently of one another, three groups of land-based animals—sirenians (manatees and their cousins), cetaceans (whales, dolphins, and porpoises), and pinnipeds (walruses, seals, and their relatives)—adapted to marine life once again. As evidence of its mammalian heritage, the manatee still has tiny nails on its paddle-like front fins (which were once its forelegs). As for hind legs? Over time, they merged to form the manatee's broad and flat tail. The manatee is a fine piece of evolutionary work!

Pachyderms—elephants, rhinos, and hippos—are this manatee's closest relatives. And like a seafaring elephant, the manatee is almost exclusively vegetarian. It's the only aquatic mammal to prefer leafy greens over living animals for meals. Eelgrass, cordgrass, turtle grass, water hyacinths—each manatee manages to munch from 32 to 108 pounds (15 to 49 kg) of this vegetation each day. All that grinding wears out a manatee's teeth, which eventually fall out. But the animal constantly grows new teeth in the back of its mouth. These teeth gradually move forward to take the place of the missing ones.

To digest its veggie diet, the manatee requires an intestinal tract that's more than 150 feet long (46 m). (A human's intestines can be up to 30 feet, or 9 m, long.) The plant material passes through the manatee's stomach and into the digestive tract, where bacteria slowly digest it. As plant fibers break down, a good amount of gas is created as a by-product—and all this gas makes a manatee very buoyant in the water. So to help the manatee to sink, its bones are pachyostotic, or solid, and act as ballast for the manatee. Its lungs also extend the length of its body to help with ballast—the air spreads out evenly, allowing the manatee to keep its body horizontal underwater. Otherwise, this air-filled animal would be like an inner tube at the swimming pool—just try to pull it completely under the surface!

CURIOUS FACT

The typical unhurried pace of a manatee is 2 to 6 miles (3 to 10 km) an hour. So that's about 3 to 9 feet (1 to 3 m) a second. Yet if agitated, it *can* kick for short bursts at a speed of 21 feet (6 m) a second. When they're active, manatees rise to the surface to breathe air once every five minutes. But when they're resting, they may take a breath only once in ten minutes.

Some giant tortoise shells angle upward in the front. This allows the tortoise to stretch its neck up to reach plants when food is scarce. This giant tortoise has access to plenty of food on the ground, so its shell is domed closer to its neck.

GALÁPAGOS GIANT TORTOISE
LIFE (ALMOST) WITHOUT PREDATION
(Chelonoidis nigra)

In 1835 the Galápagos tortoise helped English naturalist Charles Darwin formulate his groundbreaking theory of evolution. During his famous voyage to the islands, he saw differences among these same tortoises, depending on which of the islands they lived. This observation, along with many others of different types of animals, led Darwin to suggest that adaptations occur over time in response to different ecosystems.

During the third of the day they are awake, giant tortoises are creatures of habit. They travel together to the same places and along the same routes. They move into the islands' shallow pools to cool off and seek relief from insects. On land they feed or dig a sandy bed for sleeping. Thousands of years of seasonal tortoise migrations inland from the shores to the lusher vegetation in the mountains have worn pathways in the islands' volcanic soil and stone. A research specialist on these tortoises, James P. Gibbs, describes them as "bulldozers."

Most Galápagos giant tortoises live to celebrate their one-hundredth birthday. But some have lived to be 170 years old! At 6 feet (2 m) long and 500 pounds (227 kg), this animal is the largest tortoise on the planet. The tortoises evolved without the stress of predators or other competitors for their plant-based diet. Some scientists suggest that this lack of competition is what allowed the tortoises to grow to their extraordinary size, a phenomenon known as gigantism. Other scientists believe that the tortoises may have been large even before they arrived at the Galápagos Islands. These scientists say that the tortoises needed to be large to survive the long, dangerous journey to the islands.

This giant tortoise can't do a respectable breaststroke or even a lousy dog paddle, but its ancestors managed to drift in the

ADAPTATION

The planet's largest tortoises are also its longest-living vertebrates (animals that have a backbone). These tortoises live on the Galápagos Islands off the coast of Ecuador in South America, where they evolved without competition or predation.

CLASSIFICATION

Kingdom: Animalia (animals)
Phylum: Chordata (chordates, or animals with a flexible rod of cells to support the body)
Subphylum: Vertebrata (true vertebrates)
Class: Reptilia (reptiles such as snakes, lizards, and turtles)
Order: Testudines (turtles)
Family: Testudinidae (turtles with high, domed shells)
Genus: *Chelonoidis* (turtles in South America and the Galápagos Islands)
Species: *C. nigra* (Galápagos giant tortoise)

Distribution: Galápagos Islands
Conservation status: Vulnerable

ocean from South America to the Galápagos Islands. Scientists think that the tortoises managed the accidental sea voyages because their extended necks allowed them to keep their heads above water and to breathe in the choppy waters. Their exceptional buoyancy likely kept them afloat as well, or they may have drifted on rafts of vegetation.

The tortoises have also evolved so they can go for a year and a half without food or water, an adaptation that would have been useful during their long sea journey to the islands. The tortoises often eat 80 pounds (36 kg) of cacti, grasses, and berries every day. Their ability to go without food and water helps them during the dry season on the islands, when food and water may be more difficult to find. The tortoises store a lot of body fat for this reason—which also explains some of that extra weight. However, that particular adaptation also contributed to the tortoise's vulnerable status. Whalers, fur sealers, and pirates in the eighteenth and nineteenth centuries caught and kept live tortoises on their ships as a source of fresh meat for their crews. Over two centuries, they killed up to two hundred thousand tortoises. Even more devastating to the population was the introduction of nonnative species to the Galápagos. Sailors who settled on the islands brought rats, pigs, goats, colonies of fire ants, and dogs to the islands. These animals reproduced over time and preyed on tortoise eggs and tortoise babies. The tortoises also had to compete with these animals for food and territory on the islands. Fewer than twenty-five thousand Galápagos giant tortoises live in the wild in the twenty-first century.

CURIOUS FACT

The giant tortoise's home turf, the Galápagos Islands, were named for the tortoises, not the other way around. Spanish explorers who came to the islands in 1535 thought the tortoise's huge shell resembled a saddle (*galapago*, in Spanish), so they gave the name to the cluster of islands, and the name stuck.

GIANT ISOPOD
DEEP-SEA GIGANTISM
(Bathynomus giganteus)

Giant isopods have two pairs of antennae, four sets of jaws, and seven pairs of legs. The first pair of legs helps move food to the jaws.

What's an isopod? you ask. Well, picture a tiny pill bug, roly-poly, sow bug, or whatever you call the woodlouse hiding under your flowerpots or stepping-stones. Rolling into a pebble-sized ball when disturbed or stretching out to half an inch (1 cm), this bug is not a bug. And even though it has a segmented hard shell, it's not related to the armored armadillo either. (Armadillos are mammals.) Nope, isopods such as the pill bug are crustaceans, animals like crayfish and crabs, which have exoskeletons—

This crustacean (an aquatic arthropod, animals with jointed limbs and a segmented body, such as a shrimp, crab, oyster, or barnacle) lives deep in the ocean and has developed its large size and sensory abilities to survive in this cold, dark habitat.

CLASSIFICATION

Kingdom: Animalia (animals)

Phylum: Arthropoda (invertebrates including insects and crustaceans with outer shells)

Subphylum: Crustacea (shrimp, crabs, lobsters, barnacles, and relatives)

Class: Malacostraca (crabs, lobsters, and relatives)

Order: Isopoda (woodlice, sea slaters, and relatives)

Family: Cirolanidae (free-swimming, marine isopods)

Genus: *Bathynomus* (giant isopods)

Species: *B. giganteus* (giant isopod)

Distribution: cold, deep waters of the Atlantic Ocean

Conservation status: Not Evaluated

skeletons on the outside of their bodies. There are thousands of species of isopods that come in many different sizes and shapes and can live on land or in the water. The small pill bug lives on land. The giant isopod lives deep in the ocean, and it is big—very big.

Most species of isopods are between 0.3 and 1 inch (0.8 to 2.5 cm) long. But through a phenomenon known as deep-sea gigantism, the giant isopod grew bigger and bigger and bigger—some are 16 inches (41 cm) long and can weigh 4 pounds (2 kg). Scientists don't know much about deep-sea gigantism or when in evolutionary history it occurred, but the phenomenon has also been seen in some squid, tube worms, and crabs. Some scientists say that the large size may help the isopod regulate its body temperature or more efficiently take in what little food is available this deep in the ocean. Others think the size is a result of the lack of competition or predators. One thing is for sure: over time, that little roly-poly's relative grew five million times heavier.

This beast typically lives about a half a mile (805 m) down in the ocean. Scientists have also seen it in the ocean from the dim light at 550 feet (167 m) to the total dark at 7,020 feet (2,140 m). Adapting to life with so little light, this creature developed huge compound eyes. Each eye has four thousand lenses that take in a piece of the view. The animal's brain quickly puts together all the visual pieces to form a single image. Even with these huge eyes, the isopod can't see very well. So it has supersensitive antennae on its head to find what little there is to eat on the bottom of the ocean floor. This includes the carcasses of dead fish, squid, and even whales. The giant isopod eats whatever it can find. Sometimes, it may ambush slow-moving creatures such as sponges and sea cucumbers. But when food is scarce, the isopod can shift into semihibernation. It buries itself in the sand and can last a few years (yes, years!) until food is more available.

Because they don't eat much, they save energy by not moving much. If the giant isopod is in danger of becoming a meal—say a tiger shark is looking for a crunchy snack—the giant isopod springs into action. These giants can strike out with four sets of jaws and seven pairs of legs. Or they can roll into a choking-hazard-sized ball—*gulp!* Either way, the tiger shark will be sorry he chose the isopod for a meal!

CURIOUS FACTS

One of the giant isopod's survival tactics has to do with reproduction. Rather than produce thousands or millions of eggs at one time—with some becoming prey—these creatures produce a limited number of offspring. The female protects her eggs until they are fully developed. Then her young emerge as small but fully formed adults.

Two other outstanding members of the deep-sea gigantism club are the giant sea squid (*Architeuthis dux*) and the giant tube worm *(Riftia pachyptila)*. The giant tube worm can reach 8 feet (2 m) long and grow 33 inches (0.8 m) in one year. Giant sea squid can grow to lengths of 59 feet (18 m).

Vampire squid are small creatures, growing to maximum lengths less than 12 inches (30 cm). Large fins at the top of the body help the squid move through the water.

VAMPIRE SQUID
LIFE IN THE PITCH-DARK SEA

(Vampyroteuthis infernalis)

Between 1,000 and 10,000 feet (305 to 3,050 m) below the ocean's surface, the deepest part of the vampire squid's habitat, the water is black as a moonless midnight. It's silent. It's cold: the temperature ranges from 36°F to 43°F (2°C to 6°C). There is little oxygen in this minimum oxygen zone.

But suddenly there's a pair of glowing, red . . . ?

You switch on your underwater flashlight. *They are eyes!* But now they're blue, and they seem to hover on a purplish-black cape of eight moving arms connected by skin. It's . . . it's . . . the vampire squid from hell! (Clever you, that's precisely what the Latin species name *infernalis* means: "from hell.")

In the ocean's minimum oxygen zone, animals and plants must develop survival tactics. Many of them are freakish adaptations. For example, to see anything in the pitch-dark sea, the vampire squid's eyes evolved to be huge.

The squid itself is nearly invisible deep in the dark ocean. When predators do come around, the squid doesn't bother squirting black ink as other squid do. That only works in environments with plenty of light. Instead, it defends itself with light. The squid's body is covered by photophores, organs that can flash light. When threatened, the squid flashes light to confuse its foe. The squid can also make and release bioluminescent (glowing) goo that dazes and stuns its predators so the squid has time to swim away.

If the bioluminescence isn't enough, the squid can use the suckers and cirri (spines) that alternate along each arm. The

ADAPTATIONS

The ratio of this squid's eye size compared to its body size is the greatest of any creature on Earth. Its eyes are one-twelfth of the squid's body length. This creature also uses bioluminescence, light produced from chemicals within its body, and it can turn itself inside out.

CLASSIFICATION

Kingdom: Animalia (animals)

Phylum: Chordata (chordates, or animals with a flexible rod of cells to support the body)

Class: Cephalopoda (squid, octopus, cuttlefish, and nautiluses)

Superorder: Octopodiformes (octopuses and vampire squid)

Order: Vampyromorphida (vampire squid)

Family: Vampyroteuthidae (vampire squid)

Genus: *Vampyroteuthis* (vampire squid)

Species: *V. infernalis* (vampire squid—the only member of its order)

Distribution: throughout the world's temperate (mild, not too hot or too cold) and tropical oceans, typically from 300 to 3,000 feet (90 to 900 m) deep

Conservation status: Not Evaluated

CURIOUS FACTS

During the Jurassic period (200 to 145.5 million years ago), many species similar to the vampire squid flourished in the ocean. The vampire squid is a phylogenetic relict, meaning it's the only surviving species in its entire classification. The order Vampyromorphida includes only this creature.

Recently, researcher Bruce Robison and his colleagues at the Monterey Bay Aquarium Research Institute (MBARI) in Moss Landing, California, discovered that the vampire squid feeds on the remains of decomposing organisms. The research team also identified two long filaments—sticky fishing line—that trail behind the squid. Particles of waste matter stick to the filaments, and the squid pulls these filaments back toward its mouth to eat the food particles it gathers.

vampire squid can actually turn itself inside out. How? It folds its arms up into an umbrella shape and retreats inside. It turns your blood cold just hearing about this, doesn't it? Just like the vampire squid's blood. Except its blood is *bright blue.*

A striped anglerfish in Indonesia blends in with its surroundings.

STRIPED ANGLERFISH
A FISH WITH TACKLE ALL ITS OWN
(Antennarius striatus)

If your habitat requires you to hunt for food in deep-sea regions where there is no light and very few passersby to eat, you'd better have a surefire lure in your tackle box. The anglerfish packs its own bait, hook, line, and pole—and a nifty superpower. It can take the shape of other animals or objects in its environment and simply wait for a gullible creature to come to the bait. Few animals use aggressive mimicry as fashionably as this species.

CLASSIFICATION

Kingdom: Animalia (animals)

Phylum: Chordata (chordates, or animals with a flexible rod of cells to support the body)

Subphylum: Vertebrata (true vertebrates)

Class: Actinopterygii (ray-finned fishes)

Order: Lophiiformes (anglerfish)

Family: Antennariidae (frogfishes, or small, tropical fish that use camouflage)

Genus: *Antennarius* (frogfishes)

Species: *A. striatus* (striped anglerfish, also known as striped frogfish, black angler, or hairy frogfish)

Distribution: throughout the world's tropical waters at depths of 3 to 656 feet (1 to 200 m)

Conservation status: Least Concern

Less than 10 inches (25 cm) long, the striped anglerfish isn't exactly what you'd call a monster of the deep, even though it looks like one. Twiglike growths waggle from the striped anglerfish's scaleless body so that it can pose as harmless seaweed or other plants. Potential prey approach, entirely unaware that this is none other than (cue the menacing soundtrack) the fish that fishes! In a classic switcheroo, the inquisitive passerby (usually a would-be predator) spots what appears to be prey—a wiggling prawn, a tempting tube worm, or some other scrumptious local tidbit. It doesn't notice that the meal it's sizing up is actually a lure dangling from a rodlike extension on the head of the anglerfish that is sizing up the passerby.

The fishing rod itself is actually the striped anglerfish's illicium, or the first of its long, fleshy dorsal (spine) fins. The tip of the illicium is the esca. This fleshy lure moves in specific patterns to look like a shrimp, worm, or small fish. What's more, the deep-sea members of the anglerfish family have bioluminescent esca—they glow in the dark. Tacky? No, essential. This shiny lure stands out in the deep, dark sea, just begging tasty fish to come closer.

CURIOUS FACT

Because the pressure in the deep sea easily exceeds more than 2,200 pounds per square inch (1,546,751 kg per sq. m), any sudden vacuum or opening fills violently with water. (You've seen a version of this in movies when luggage and passengers in airplanes are sent flying as a door opens or a wall is punctured.) That same type of pressure is key to the anglerfish's finishing move with prey: its jaws snap open in a mere six milliseconds—one of the fastest moves in all of nature. This quick work creates so much suction that rushing water sweeps the prey on the esca into the fish's mouth and at the same time expands the volume of the anglerfish's mouth to twelve times its normal size. (That blast must feel like swallowing a waterfall! A teensy one, but still.) As the water then exits through the anglerfish's gills, the suction pulls the prey on its way down to the anglerfish's stomach, which, quite conveniently, can also expand to digest creatures twice its size.

A striped anglerfish opens its mouth wide to suck in its prey. The fish's illicium and esca are well camouflaged, but the thick esca is visible above its mouth.

This fishing fish is even built for the one that got away. Should a predator gobble up the bait without being hooked, the anglerfish can regenerate a new lure, dust itself off, and start all over again.

A mantis strikes a pose to fend off its enemies.

DEVIL'S FLOWER MANTIS
FLORAL ASSASSIN (Idolomantis diabolica)

When a devil's flower mantis holds a pose among the petals of a flower (imagine nature hitting the Pause button), it's practically invisible. That's a good thing for the mantis. It's not so good for any insect that approaches to gather pollen or slurp nectar.

The devil's flower mantis, at 4 to 5 inches (10 to 13 cm) long, is the largest of the praying mantises. (The name comes from the folded prayerlike position of their arms.) Mantises are carnivores, or meat eaters, so the one that really needs to be praying is the prey. A frozen-still mantis may appear harmless when its spiked front legs are folded in, but those lethal weapons (imagine nature hitting the Fast-Forward button now) are poised to quickly spear, slice, dice, and chop.

When threatened, the mantis will rise up and stretch its forelegs overhead to appear even larger. Then it gives up the praying-monk disguise and turns into a samurai warrior with a pair of raised swords.

Yes, there's something devilish about this predator. Gradually, after it hatches, a mantis's legs lengthen and the immature mantis transforms. With each molting, a mantis outgrows its carapace, typically about seven or eight times before it is fully grown. A young mantis looks like brown, dead leaves. An adult has bright, vibrant colors to blend in with the surrounding flowers and plants. A mature adult can resemble its host flower so much— even swaying along with a breeze—

ADAPTATION

This insect exhibits two stages of camouflaging disguise. At birth, to escape the notice of predators (including older mantises), it is shiny and black to look like an ant. Then, as an adult, it changes its outward appearance several times, molting (shedding the external carapace, or shell) until it resembles the flowers and leaves it lives among.

CLASSIFICATION

Kingdom: Animalia (animals)
Phylum: Arthropoda (invertebrates with outer shells, including insects, shellfish, spiders, and relatives)
Class: Insecta (insects)
Order: Mantodea (mantids)
Family: Empusidae (plant-mimicking mantids)
Genus: *Idolomantis* (devil's flower mantids)
Species: *I. diabolica* (devil's flower mantis)

Distribution: African countries of Kenya, Malawi, Ethiopia, Somalia, Tanzania, and Uganda
Conservation status: Not Evaluated

that the mantis's prey will make an effort to pollinate it. And die trying! There's no mistaking this beauty for anything other than what it is: an assassin.

The devil's flower mantis has compound eyes and a wide range of vision. This allows the mantis to see predators and prey without moving and giving up its position.

CURIOUS FACT

The root word of *mantis* comes from the Greek word for "prophet," a seer with spiritual powers. This insect is the subject of dozens of myths. In various cultures, the mantis is said to have the ability to point pilgrims toward Islam's holy city of Mecca in Saudi Arabia. Some African myths say it can find lost livestock, and in France, it is said to find lost children. In China its eggs are said to spare a child the embarrassment of bedwetting. In North America, it's said to blind people and subdue a horse with a spray of brown juice from its jaws. Or not.

Some people have said that the bristles on bobbit worms can sting or even paralyze other creatures and humans. Some similar worms do have toxic bristles, but scientists have found that bobbit worms do not use their bristles for defense.

BOBBIT WORM
A CARNIVORE'S SPEED
(Eunice aphroditois)

At Newquay's Blue Reef Aquarium, in Cornwall, England, staff members repeatedly found maimed fish and broken chunks of coral in one of their display tanks. To catch whatever was devouring the tank mates, the staff set out baited hooks. In the morning, both bait and hooks were gone. So the aquarium staff took the tank apart and found a predator sea worm that was almost 4 feet (1 m) long. They named it Barry—and quickly gave Barry its own tank.

Even in your worst nightmare, you probably don't want to hear the word *predator* linked to *worm*. But imagine if it were nighttime, 30 or even 130 feet (9 or 40 m) down on the ocean floor where the Indian and Pacific Oceans meet. You are an unsuspecting fish, and you live in a world where this sea monster—yes, it's a monster—can grow up to 10 feet (3 m) long from the tip of its five antennae to the last segment of its body. And each segment has paired legs called parapodia (from the Latin words *para*, for "beside," and *podia*, for "feet"). Each parapodia is covered in bristles that the worm uses to grip the sand to help it move or stay in place when it is buried.

If you live your life buried in the sand, when something edible swims by, you need to seize the opportunity. So this bristle worm will eat just about anything it can find, including fish, other worms, and plants. When hunting, it uses ambush techniques. Its body glints purple and red as if its skin were made of gemstones. Its antennae can detect chemicals or changes in light from nearby organisms. When they sense that something edible is nearby or is admiring its fancy colors, the worm leaps out and shoots its pharynx forward (that's the part of the digestive tract right behind the mouth and throat). The pharynx turns inside out to seize the meal with the sharp-toothed jaws at its end.

It's like an undersea jack-in-the-box with the power of a *T. rex*. Once it has its prey, it injects the animal with a paralyzing toxin—*poof!* Then it drags the meal in a cloud of bottom muck and sand into its private dining room on the ocean floor. Let the nightmares begin!

CURIOUS FACT

These marine worms are not frequently observed in the wild, so scientists are still uncertain how to classify them. To study them, researchers preserve them in various chemicals. These chemicals often cause the animals to lose their distinctive coloration. Differences in color can often be the deciding factor that leads scientists to classify two individuals as members of separate species or of the same one.

The bobbit senses its surroundings using its five striped antennae. Below the antennae, its wide jaws wait to seize prey.

CAMEL SPIDER
THE LARGEST (INVERTEBRATE) JAWS IN THE DESERT (Solifugae)

When US soldiers were stationed in the Middle East in the 1990s and early 2000s, the camel spider achieved its fifteen minutes of fame. Soldiers posted photos of themselves on the Internet with various ginormous camel spiders. (The spiders are actually fairly small, but through macro photography—or extreme close-ups—

you can hold something close to a camera's lens and snap the shutter to get a photo that will make that object seem huge.) The accompanying stories included the "facts" that this leaping monster was as big as a dinner plate and fed on camels. As you might guess, none of these stories was true.

Camel spiders—there are 1,075 different species—are also known as wind scorpions, sun spiders, and solifuges. (*Solifuge* comes from the Latin words *solis*, meaning "sun," and *fuge*, for "fleeing." As you might guess, these spiders live in the shade.) Most of them are small enough to fit in your hand. But others are much larger, growing to more than 6 inches (15 cm) long. Camel spiders belong to the class Arachnida, a group that includes scorpions, mites, and spiders. They all have eight legs, and they don't have wings or antennae. Unlike true spiders, camel spiders don't spin webs or inject venom into their prey. (You definitely don't want to sit across from a camel spider in the lunchroom. They're messy eaters.)

Camel spiders appear to have ten legs, but the first pair aren't really legs. They are pedipalps and are a type of feeler with sticky tips similar to tiny suction cups. The spider holds the pedipalps outward, not touching the ground. They guide the spider through obstacles and help it detect and grab onto prey.

ADAPTATIONS

Neither camel nor spider, this creature has unique suction-like organs on the tips of its first set of feelers for seizing scarce prey in the desert. And it manages to spray digestive juices onto its victims before eating them. Nice!

CLASSIFICATION

Kingdom: Animalia (animals)
Phylum: Arthropoda (invertebrates with outer shells: insects, shellfish, spiders, and relatives)
Class: Arachnida (spiders, scorpions, mites, and others)
Subclass: Dromopoda (scorpions, pseudoscorpions, and daddy longlegs)
Order: Solifugae (camel spiders, divided into twelve families and 140 genera)

Distribution: most deserts except in Australia
Conservation status: Not Evaluated

Once the spider has snatched its prey, the chelicerae—two claw- or fang-like mouthparts—grate and mince the prey. Since it doesn't have venom, the spider needs the chelicerae in case its prey tries to turn into a predator. (For their size, camel spiders have the largest jaws of any invertebrate on land.) Finally, the camel spider sprays digestive juices onto the victim, which quickly dissolves into a protein shake that the spider can slurp down with a satisfied *ahh*!

CURIOUS FACTS

The camel spider has eight legs plus pedipalps—for eating, climbing, drinking (bringing water up to its mouth), and mating (holding the female in place). The first set of legs are also used to sense the environment. The spider uses its remaining six legs for moving around. And even with only six legs, the spider can manage a 10-mile-an-hour (16 km) sprint.

Camel spiders are sometimes known as *haarskeerders* or *baardskeerders* (meaning "hair cutters" and "beard cutters," respectively) in Afrikaans, a language in South Africa. In South Africa, some believe that solifuges line their underground lairs with human hair that they apparently snip with their chelicerae from humans unaware of the theft.

Tasmanian devils can open their mouths wide. It looks fierce but is more likely an expression of fear.

TASMANIAN DEVIL
A RARE CARNIVOROUS MARSUPIAL
(Sarcophilus harrisii)

The Tasmanian devil's loud growling, fanatical lunging, teeth baring, and frantic shredding may seem like the actions of maniacs or demons. Their table manners even inspired the *Looney Tunes* cartoon character Taz, whose frenzied whirling actions, well, weren't all that exaggerated!

With the massive neck and mouth of a great white shark and the body of a wombat, this stocky devil is like the prehistoric saber-toothed tiger of the Americas. But it lives on the Australian

ADAPTATIONS

The Tasmanian devil is the planet's largest meat-eating marsupial. (These mammals, which include kangaroos, opossums, and wallabies, carry their young in an abdominal pouch.) And its jaws have the greatest bite force compared to body size of any living creature on Earth.

CLASSIFICATION

Kingdom: Animalia (animals)

Phylum: Chordata (chordates, or animals with a flexible rod of cells to support the body)

Subphylum: Vertebrata (true vertebrates)

Class: Mammalia (mammals)

Subclass: Prototheria (egg-laying mammals—echidnas and platypus)

Infraclass: Marsupialia (marsupials)

Order: Dasyuromorphia (Australian carnivorous marsupials)

Family: Dasyuridae (small, mouselike marsupials)

Genus: *Sarcophilus* (Tasmanian devil and two other extinct species)

Species: *S. harrisii* (Tasmanian devil)

Distribution: Tasmania, an Australian island state off the southern coast of Australia

Conservation status: Endangered

island of Tasmania. Up to 30 inches (76 cm) long and about 26 pounds (12 kg), it's the world's largest meat-eating marsupial. Adapting to a life of meat eating requires a mighty set of chompers to cut through organs, muscles, fur, and bones.

The Taz's bite is among the fiercest of any mammal. Its jaws have more power than animals twice or even four times its size. For instance, the average dog bite exerts about 320 pounds per square inch (224,982 kg per sq. m) of force. Meanwhile, the Taz delivers an incredible 5,100 pounds per square inch (3,585,655 kg per sq. m).

What's more, the Taz's teeth continue to grow throughout its six years of life. On a typical day, the Taz consumes 15 percent of its body weight, or 4 pounds (2 kg). On a more unusual day, one devil can down 10 pounds (4.5 kg) of food in thirty minutes. That's 40 percent of its body weight. To compare, if you weigh 100 pounds (45 kg), that would be the equivalent of eating 40 pounds (18 kg)—or 1.3 pounds (0.6 kg) every minute for thirty minutes. That's like eating a large Thanksgiving turkey, the stuffing, and all the typical side dishes—by yourself!

CURIOUS FACTS

Tasmanian devils are scavengers, eating anything that comes their way. And since the Taz will eat the whole carcass of an animal—meat, fur, and bones—they are considered landscape hygienists, removing vast amounts of roadkill and washed-up fish from the island.

In the mid-1990s, an outbreak of a fatal cancer spread among the Tasmanian devil population. The disease causes an eruption of swellings and lumps around the head and mouth, and affected animals gradually starve. Because of the disease, the Tasmanian devil is listed as endangered and vulnerable, with fewer than ten thousand to twenty-five thousand mature animals remaining in the wild. Scientists are working to develop a treatment for the disease.

Some people in Tasmania think devils are pests, but farmers appreciate devils because they kill rodents, keeping them from destroying crops.

In African folklore, the marabou stork was created using all the leftover bits after the other animals were made. The stories say that this is the reason for the stork's odd appearance.

MARABOU STORK
A SCAVENGER'S LIFE

(Leptoptilos crumeniferus)

One of the largest terrestrial birds, marabou storks have hollow legs and toe bones. This makes it easier for them to get airborne. In flight they also bring their necks in toward their shoulders the way herons do. This posture puts some of the weight of the beak on the shoulders, making flight easier and more efficient.

The birds are commonly known as undertaker birds. That's because they sport a black cloak of wings and a nearly bald head. It's a look that suits a scavenger that's constantly hacking into carcasses with its huge bill. The bill ranges from 10 to almost 14 inches (26 to 35 cm) long. It works like a scalpel or scraper to whack off bits of innards it can swallow whole. It sounds like something from a horror movie, but the marabou stork is actually something of a health-care professional. Its bald head and neck are key for hygiene, for example. And as a scavenger, it gets rid of rotting carcasses, helping to eliminate diseases that could be harmful to both animals and humans. Hacking up a tough hide gives other scavengers with smaller tools the chance to partake in the carcass.

Marabou storks dine on dead things, but they'll make an exception to eat live fish, insects, pigeons, flamingos, and crocodile hatchlings. Such a diverse menu isn't surprising—an adult stork needs more than 1.5 pounds (0.7 kg) of food every day. Its eclectic diet even motivates marabou storks to snatch up animals running from forest fires. The storks are also spotted scoping out butcher shops, fishing villages, and dumps, looking for scraps. Undertaking this bird's life is ugh-ly business!

ADAPTATION

With a wingspan up to 13 feet (4 m) wide, these 20-pound (9 kg) wading birds evolved into the largest scavenging bird in Africa— second in size only to the condor of South America. When it comes to food, even vultures know to give these large birds first dibs.

CLASSIFICATION

Kingdom: Animalia (animals)
Phylum: Chordata (chordates, or animals with a flexible rod of cells to support the body)
Subphylum: Vertebrata (true vertebrates)
Class: Aves (all birds)
Order: Ciconiiformes (storks and relatives)
Family: Ciconiidae (storks)
Genus: *Leptoptilos* (marabou and adjutant storks)
Species: *L. crumeniferus* (marabou stork)

Distribution: riverbanks, lakeshores, and savannas (grasslands) of sub-Saharan Africa
Conservation status: Least Concern

A marabou stork soars thousands of feet high while it searches for food below. It is recognizable in flight by the way its legs trail behind it.

Pelicans are not able to flap their wings for very long during flight. Instead, they spread their wings to soar through the air. When landing, the wings also act as brakes to slow the birds down as they glide toward the water.

AUSTRALIAN PELICAN
(Pelecanus conspicillatus)
LIFE AS A HEAVYWEIGHT FLIER

The bird bill is the stuff of legends. A toucan's bill is multicolored and spans up to half of the bird's body length. A hornbill's is curved and helmeted. And a stork's bill is most legendary of all, for carrying human babies. But what can fit more fish in its bill and knock them back without a knife and fork? The Australian pelican!

With an 8-foot (2.4 m) wingspan, a bill that often exceeds 1.5 feet (0.5 m) long, and a body that measures 6 feet (2 m) from the tip of its bill to the edge of its tail feathers, Australian pelicans are among the world's heaviest fliers. They typically tip the scales at 30 pounds (14 kg). Thanks to evolutionary adaptation, they also possess extreme skeletal pneumaticity. Most bones have small, honeycomb-like pockets of air in them. In pneumatic bones, these pockets are expanded air sacs. The bones are thin and hollow but also strong and stiff. (Think about aircraft: the key is to use the lightest materials with the greatest strength.)

The bones of an Australian pelican make up less than 10 percent, or 3 pounds (1 kg), of the bird's total weight. (An adult human's 206 skeletal bones are usually 15 percent of body weight. The bones are not pneumatic, so they have more mass and are heavier.) With such lightweight bones, this hefty aviator can manage continuous flight for twenty-four hours. It takes advantage of thermals (warm air drafts that rise from Earth into the cooler atmosphere above) to soar as high as 2 miles (3 km) above the water. Using minimal energy, the pelicans can move at speeds up to 35 miles (56 km) an hour.

When it's time to refuel, the Australian pelican skims the water, flying just a few feet above the waves to spot a likely meal. Unlike most pelicans, which mostly eat fish, this species regularly eats insects and shellfish, reptiles and amphibians, and even species of gulls and ducks. Plunging its bill into the sea, the pelican nets

The Australian pelican's bill is the largest of any bird, reaching up to 20 inches (51 cm) in length. The bill has a hook on the end to help grab slippery fish.

its meal with its gular pouch, or expandable throat, and clamps its bill shut. Then it squeezes the pouch against its chest to push out the water—more than 3 gallons (11 L) in a swallow—to line up its dinner, head down, for a smooth slide down the hatch.

CURIOUS FACT

Australian pelicans are cooperative hunters. Dozens, hundreds, or even thousands (the largest group ever witnessed was two thousand strong) of pelicans work together to find fish to eat. They scare schooling fish into shallower water or tighter and tighter circles by stirring up the water with their bills and wings. When the fish are in a small enough area, the pelicans plunge in and swallow the prey in an all-you-can-fit-in-your-stomach buffet. Talk about a winning survival strategy!

SKELETAL PNEUMATICITY

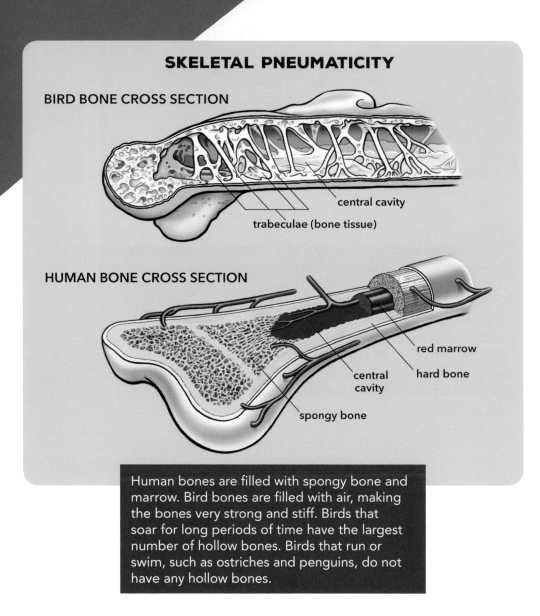

BIRD BONE CROSS SECTION

central cavity

trabeculae (bone tissue)

HUMAN BONE CROSS SECTION

red marrow

central cavity

hard bone

spongy bone

Human bones are filled with spongy bone and marrow. Bird bones are filled with air, making the bones very strong and stiff. Birds that soar for long periods of time have the largest number of hollow bones. Birds that run or swim, such as ostriches and penguins, do not have any hollow bones.

Not only is the tapir's nose useful for life in the forest, but its whole body is shaped to help it move through the habitat. The tapir is narrower in the front than the back so it can more easily navigate through thick plants.

MALAYAN TAPIR
A MOST NOTEWORTHY NOSE *(Tapirus indicus)*

Oh, beast of the prodigious proboscis! (*Proboscis* comes from the Greek word *proboskis*, which translates to "a means for taking food.") The tapir is most active at dawn and dusk, when there's not much light. And its tiny eyes don't exactly provide the best eyesight. So this creature has to rely on its nose to find its way through the dense forests where it lives. Flexible like the trunk of an elephant (curiously, the trunkless rhinos and horses are the tapir's closer cousins), the tapir's extended nose can perform a multitude of functions for its vegetarian life. It can snatch fallen fruit from the forest floor. It can grab branches of higher foliage. Most crucially, by lifting its snout, baring its teeth, and inhaling, it can sniff the urine-marked paths of other tapirs that crisscross its territory. Because each tapir's foraging ground covers a very large territory—including bodies of water—it often overlaps that of other tapirs. Urine is a way to mark territory to maintain the boundaries that allow animals to give one another some space. Scent marks are a first warning to competitors: *Come any closer, and . . .*

Oh, odd-toed ungulate! (You know, a hooved mammal.) A tapir's forelegs have four toes (only three touch the ground), and its rear legs have three. All are splayed to support the tapir's heavy body on muddy terrain or hillsides—or on the bottom of a soggy riverbed.

Oh, snorkel-snouted sniffer! The tapir can close off its nostrils, sink to the river bottom, and continue to graze vegetation there for up to ninety seconds. A tapir can swim too, head above water or just under it, extending the proboscis into the air to work like a snorkel.

And while its jaws can deliver a nasty bite in a fight, the tapir prefers to flee. If a tiger or leopard appears threatening, the tapir

ADAPTATION

This mammal has a prominent snout with a remarkable range of abilities. It tracks scents, works like a snorkel, and lifts objects the way an elephant's trunk does.

CLASSIFICATION

Kingdom: Animalia (animals)
Phylum: Chordata (chordates, or animals with a flexible rod of cells to support the body)
Subphylum: Vertebrata (true vertebrates)
Class: Mammalia (mammals)
Order: Perissodactyla (odd-toed ungulates: horses, tapirs, and rhinoceroses)
Family: Tapiridae (tapirs)
Genus: *Tapirus* (tapirs)
Species: *T. indicus* (Malayan tapir)

Distribution: Southeast Asia, including parts of Indonesia, Malaysia, Thailand, and Myanmar
Conservation status: Endangered

will sink underwater and hold its breath until the great cat proves to be a scaredy-cat and gives up on having tapir tenderloin for supper.

Should a predator lunge onto its neck, the tapir has thick skin to provide some protection. But according to an 1834 issue of the *American Magazine of Useful and Entertaining Knowledge*, "The Tapir rushes into the thick woods, and endeavors to kill his assailant by dashing him against some large tree."

CURIOUS FACTS

This two-toned tapir—a black hide with a large white saddle—is entirely designed for the dim light of its forest home. The black-and-white pattern camouflages the tapir. Because its dark skin is difficult to see in the dark, predators only see the white parts. These, on their own, don't look like the outline of an animal. Scientists call this adaptive strategy disruptive coloration.

The length and flexibility of a tapir's penis allows the male to direct its urine behind it. This is hardly a unique trait to tapirs: lions, raccoons, hippos, and camels also urinate backward. But one thing *is* unique to tapirs: they can aim and shoot their urine as far as 16 feet (5 m).

A tapir sinks into the water, keeping its nose up to breathe.

Naked mole rats can move their incisors independently in a motion similar to eating with chopsticks.

NAKED MOLE RAT
MAMMALS LIVING LIKE ANTS (*Heterocephalus glaber*)

Naked—aren't all creatures?—but neither a mole nor a rat, this 3-inch (7.6 cm), barely haired beastie is a relative of porcupines and guinea pigs. You might argue that they have more in common with insects.

Mole rats are the only mammals that live the way ants and bees do, in a community that's considered eusocial. (The prefix *eu* comes from the Greek word for "real" or "true.") In this type of community, members contribute in various ways to the creation and survival of the next generation. A naked mole rat colony will easily count three hundred individuals. They include one breeding female, a few males with which she mates, and lots of nonbreeders that do all the digging, feeding, tending of the young, and defending of the homestead. The female has litters of pups up to five times in a year, and each litter can have as many as twenty-eight newborns. While that *is* the largest litter size of any mammal, fewer than a dozen of the babies will live past weaning (when an animal first eats food other than its mother's milk).

The entire colony lives underground in a complex of tunnels that can stretch for 1 mile (1.6 km) or more and up to 8 feet (2.4 m) deep. Lining up nose to tail, the mole rat construction crew forms something like a bucket brigade. A digger gnaws into fresh soil, sweepers kick the dirt backward, backward, backward, and finally a "volcano-er" bucks the dirt out of the hole in a mound of not-so-hot lava.

Without excavators and shovels, the mole rats' mouths have evolved to do the heavy lifting. One-quarter of the mole rat's muscles are in its jaws, and its large incisors stick out of the lips to cut into the soil. These naked creatures actually *do* have hair—inside their mouths. These bristly hairs keep dirt out of the mouth while the mole rat munches

ADAPTATION

The naked mole rat lives underground in a social society. The members accomplish different tasks for the good of the group as a whole. This behavior protects the naked mole rats from predators and helps them reproduce, find food and water, and live long lives in the desert, a challenging habitat where food and water are scarce.

CLASSIFICATION

Kingdom: Animalia (animals)
Phylum: Chordata (chordates, or animals with a flexible rod of cells to support the body)
Subphylum: Vertebrata (true vertebrates)
Class: Mammalia (mammals)
Order: Rodentia (rodents including mice, rats, squirrels, beavers, porcupines, and relatives)
Family: Bathyergidae (mole rats and blesmols)
Subfamily: Heterocephalinae (naked mole rats)
Genus: *Heterocephalus* (naked mole rat)
Species: *H. glaber* (naked mole rat, or desert mole rat)

Distribution: East Africa (Ethiopia, Somalia, and Kenya)
Conservation status: Least Concern

CURIOUS FACTS

Ants, bees, aphids, as well as some wasps, termites, and beetles are all eusocial—the highest form of social organization among animals. Only two vertebrates are eusocial: the naked mole rat and another burrowing rodent, the Damaraland blesmol (*Fukomys damarensis*), which lives in the deserts and grasslands of southern Africa.

Mole rats live with limited supplies of oxygen. Because their tunnels are so crowded, it is difficult for carbon dioxide to exit and fresh oxygen to enter. So mole rat blood has adapted to be extra efficient and take in whatever oxygen is present.

through the soil with its teeth.

The mole rat's mouth is well developed, but its eyes are essentially sightless. They also can't regulate their own body heat or feel pain. But let's be honest, is any of that stuff really necessary? A mole rat spends its thirty years of life in the pitch-black underground huddled up with three hundred of its closest friends. These sand puppies, as they're known in the deserts of East Africa where they live, are perfectly adapted to underground life.

Sloths are the only mammals with hair that grows in the opposite direction from other mammals. It grows up from the belly toward the back so that rain can more easily flow off the animals in a rainstorm.

TWO-TOED SLOTH
UPSIDE DOWN AND COATED WITH ALGAE
(Choloepus didactylus)

A rolling stone gathers no moss, right? Well, this animal proves that proverb to be true but in reverse. The button-eyed, tiny-eared, small-brained, round-headed sloth—the planet's pokiest mammal—rolls around so little that moss—algae, actually—grows in its fur. Each hair on a sloth is grooved and absorbs water, creating an ideal environment for algae. In fact, the sloth's fur hosts an entire mini-ecosystem where cockroaches, beetles, and moths live off the algae. The algae also camouflage the sloth's dark body from predators. And the algae provide a bit of a food source for its young.

This little ecosystem spends most of its life upside down. Females even give birth upside down! The sloth's curved claws are 3 to 4 inches (8 to 10 cm) long. They have two on each of their hands and three on each of their feet. They hook these claws onto a thick branch and, basically, hang on tight. Sloths sleep upside down too—for nearly eighteen hours a day. (If you've ever wondered why laziness is known as sloth, you've got your answer.)

For a life of eating leaves, a sloth's mouth is built for grinding. Its lips perform like incisors: they are tough and can shred and rip leaves. The sloth's molars grow continuously since chewing on tough leaves all the time wears down the tooth's surface.

But for all this shredding and grinding, sloths get very little energy from leaves. To adapt to this lack of calories, a sloth has an extremely low body temperature, ranging from 74°F to 92°F (24°C to 33°C). For comparison, a human's healthy body temperature is 98.6°F (37°C). The sloth also has an extremely slow metabolism. For example, it can take a month for a sloth's body to break down a big serving of foliage.

About two-thirds of a sloth's weight is the contents of its huge, compartmentalized stomach. Some of that weight is also water. Leaves provide the only water a sloth drinks. About once a week, the sloth comes down for a bathroom break. It drags itself (a sloth's back legs are so weak that it isn't able to stand or walk) to the same spot every time, digs a hole, does its business, and covers up the spot. Sloths can't flee from jaguars and other predators. These sluggers can bite, hiss, screech, slash, and gash instead.

CURIOUS FACTS

Sloths are excellent swimmers. Sometimes they'll drop into the water below to swim to a different tree. And no, they don't swim upside down in a backstroke—it's a rather sloppy, sloshy dog paddle with their forelimbs. Still, that stroke propels them through the water three times faster than the sloth can move on land. And they can hold a single breath for up to forty minutes.

The algae that grow on a sloth's body is specific to the sloth. It exists nowhere else in nature. According to Milla Suutari, lead researcher of the Department of Environmental Science at the University of Helsinki, in Finland, "Found only in sloth hair [this alga] . . . is passed directly from the mother to the offspring." The algae receive water and shelter from the sloth, and the sloth receives camouflage and additional nutrients that absorb into its skin. It's a classic definition of a symbiotic, or mutually beneficial, relationship.

Proboscis monkeys are named for their long, fleshy noses. The nose amplifies the monkey's calls so it can threaten its rivals or warn fellow monkeys of danger.

PROBOSCIS MONKEY
A PRIMATE THAT'S IN THE SWIM
(Nasalis larvatus)

The nose knows when it comes to the proboscis monkey! While the females do have unusually large schnozzles, it's the males that possess a truly impressive proboscis, or nasal appendage. Their noses can be 7 inches (18 cm) long, a length that can be one-quarter of the monkey's entire body length. The monkeys are mainly folivores (leaf eaters) and frugivores (fruit eaters). At mealtimes one hand has to swing the nose aside to make way for the other hand to deliver the food to the animal's lips.

So why such a pendulous proboscis? It's not for stronger sniffing. Instead, it's to amplify the animal's vocalization, or calls. The large nose creates a chamber that allows space for the monkey's growls, toots, and squeaks to vibrate and become louder. When the proboscis monkey is distressed, angry, or excited, extra blood flows to the nose. This causes the already large nose to swell even larger, making even more space to turn up the volume and intensity of the sounds. In fact, a really urgent honk can even send the nose farther outward—not exactly like a New Year's Eve noisemaker that unrolls when you blow through it . . . but kind of.

Proboscis monkeys use their nasal noises to threaten rivals and defend territory. Females also find the bigger, blushing, bulbous noses attractive. Across the animal kingdom, a male's show of size, color, action, or strength demonstrates that he is a good choice of mate. Females are biologically attracted to these displays of fitness. They sense that a fit male will contribute good genes to their offspring. His strength or status within their monkey troop will also ensure the survival of his family.

ADAPTATIONS

This creature is one of the few primates that can swim. It's also the only one with a large nose that has evolved to make its calls and alarms louder.

CLASSIFICATION

Kingdom: Animalia (animals)
Phylum: Chordata (chordates, or animals with a flexible rod of cells to support the body)
Subphylum: Vertebrata (true vertebrates)
Class: Mammalia (mammals)
Order: Primates (primates)
Family: Cercopithecidae (Old World monkeys)
Subfamily: Colobinae (colobus monkeys, leaf monkeys, and relatives)
Genus: *Nasalis* (proboscis monkey)
Species: *N. larvatus* (proboscis monkey, or Dutch monkey)

Distribution: forests on the island nation of Borneo in Southeast Asia
Conservation status: Endangered

In the proboscis monkey's realm, adult males host a harem (a group of females associated with one male) of admirers. They live together in a large troop with as many as seventy-five or more individuals. These marshland primates are arboreal—they feed, sleep, play, and mate among trees. To avoid a leopard, they can leap from a tree limb into a river below and swim more than 20 yards (18 m) in a single breath.

CURIOUS FACT

Proboscis monkeys not only have noticeable noses, but they also have sizable stomachs. Their stomachs have several sections, which contain bacteria to help break down the tough fibers of the plants that make up the monkeys' diet. One-quarter of the monkey's weight is food that's being digested. Males average between 35 and 51 pounds (16 and 23 kg). Females weigh less than half that. So a male's belly might hold something like 9 to 13 pounds (4 to 6 kg) of decomposing vegetation. You might think of these animals as tree-dwelling cows—but in a monkey suit.

A mole cricket's front legs have bladelike projections known as dactyls. Differences in the dactyls help distinguish different species of mole cricket.

MOLE CRICKET
AN INSECT WITH CLAWS (Gryllotalpidae)

So what are a mole's mitts doing on the ends of an insect's forearms, you might wonder? Did nature get its wires crossed? Well, no. Every species on Earth comes up with survival strategies for its particular environment. Sometimes vastly different creatures independently evolve a similar strategy for survival. The digging claw of the mole and of the mole cricket is a fine example of this evolutionary concept, called convergent evolution.

Through natural selection, mole crickets, like the mammalian mole, developed a tool for life underground: powerful mitts perfect for digging. Tunneling underground provides access to food sources—stems, roots, and tubers. It also offers safe nesting burrows, escape routes, and chambers for mating and molting.

Mole crickets use their enormous claws—part garden trowel, part steam-shovel bucket—to excavate about 20 feet (6 m) of tunnel every night. For a creature that's less than 2 inches (5 cm) long, we're talking truly extraordinary excavation expertise! Major mining mojo! Spectacular scooping skills! Along the way, the moles nibble on roots, dislodge surface vegetation, and create dead patches in lawns—*oops*.

Able to dig, run, fly, and swim, mole crickets are so successful that they're viewed as a major garden pest throughout much of the world. Except in East Asia. There, these diggers are served deep-fried to a delectable crispness and accompanied with sticky rice!

ADAPTATION
This insect developed claws that look and function like those of the mammalian mole.

CLASSIFICATION
Kingdom: Animalia (animals)
Class: Insecta (insects)
Order: Orthoptera (grasshoppers, katydids, locusts, crickets, and relatives)
Suborder: Ensifera (the "long-horned grasshoppers": crickets, katydids, and relatives)
Family: Gryllotalpidae (mole crickets)
Genus: *Gryllotalpa* (mole crickets)

Distribution: every continent except Antarctica
Conservation status: varies among species; Least Concern for some species; many species with insufficient data for evaluation

CURIOUS FACTS

The male mole cricket uses his tunnel as a megaphone. He rubs his wings together in the entrance of the tunnel, creating a chirpy click. The sound is amplified by the tunnel—music to the female mole cricket's ears as she uses sound to locate a mate.

Crickets have an extremely elaborate system of hearing mechanisms that allow them to pick up sounds and vibrations from both near and far. Twenty-seven sense organs called crista acustica are located along the midleg and hind leg. Working together, they help the insect detect from where and how far away a sound is coming.

Mole crickets often tunnel just underneath the surface, leaving trails of pushed-up soil similar to those of mammalian moles.

FRILL-NECKED LIZARD

DRAGON ON TWO LEGS

(Chlamydosaurus kingii)

This "dragon" lives in the trees of Australia. And despite its lack of magical powers, it is still the continent's beloved national treasure. The frill-necked, or frilled, lizard hangs out in trees much of the day, taking in heat from the sunshine. It's an ectotherm that must get warmth from its environment. Because ectotherms don't make their own heat, they don't have to eat as much or as often as some other creatures do to get energy. Many ectotherms sit and wait for their prey so they can use less energy for finding food. The frill-necked lizard will leave its warm perch every now and then to ambush butterflies and moths, chase little lizards or, during the wet season, binge on ants or termites.

When threatened by a dingo, feral cat, or bird of prey (or when courting a mate), this 1-foot-long (0.3 m) lizard lashes its whip of a tail across the ground. Its frill—a ruffle of skin that usually lies flat around its shoulders—opens wide around its head. Then it hisses and thrusts open its mouth to bare its menacing teeth and to reveal its bright pink or yellow throat. The lizard may also choose to lunge toward its predator or appear to begin a chase.

Scared? If not, the frilly dragon has one more battle plan. It can stand upright on its hind legs and hightail it to the nearest tree. Literally—it raises its tail and forelegs high off the ground as it runs away. This, it seems, causes the predator to giggle rather than pursue.

SOURCE NOTES

7. Serina Golden, "Elegance in Science," *Inside Higher Ed*, July 14, 2010, https://www.insidehighered.com/news/2010/07/14/glynn.

11. Emma Marris, "Genetics Probe Identifies New Galapagos Tortoise Species," *Nature*, October 21, 2015, http://www.nature.com/news/genetics-probe-identifies-new-galapagos-tortoise-species-1.18611.

21. Krijn Michel, quoted in James Urquhart, "Tongues May Have Evolved from a Mouthful of Water," *New Scientist*, March 18, 2015, https://www.newscientist.com/article/dn27181-tongues-may-have-evolved-from-a-mouthful-of-water.

33. Doug Stewart, "Making Sense of Manatees," *National Wildlife*, April 1, 1999, http://www.nwf.org/News-and-Magazines/National-Wildlife/Animals/Archives/1999/Making-Sense-of-Manatees.aspx.

37. Elahe Izadi, "The 'Peculiar' History behind Science's Race to Bring Extinct Tortoises Back to Life," *Washington Post*, December 18, 2015, https://www.washingtonpost.com/news/speaking-of-science/wp/2015/12/18/the-peculiar-history-behind-sciences-race-to-bring-extinct-tortoises-back-to-life.

69. Nathaniel Hawthorne and Elizabeth Manning Hawthorne, *American Magazine of Useful and Entertaining Knowledge*, vol. 1 (Boston: Boston Bewick, 1835), 47.

75. Milla Suutari et al., "Molecular Evidence for a Diverse Green Algal Community Growing in the Hair of Sloths and a Specific Association with *Trichophilus welckeri* (Chlorophyta, Ulvophyceae)," *BMC Evolutionary Biology*, March 30, 2010, https://bmcevolbiol.biomedcentral.com/articles/10.1186/1471-2148-10-86.

GLOSSARY

amphibian: a cold-blooded vertebrate, such as a frog, salamander, or newt. It has an aquatic juvenile form, equipped with gills that can absorb oxygen from water, and a terrestrial adult form, possessing lungs to breathe oxygen from the air.

ballast system: in zoology, structures and processes that help an animal rise, sink, or maintain its position in water

biome: a large, naturally occurring community of flora and fauna occupying a major habitat, for example, forest or tundra

bipedalism: the ability to stand and walk on two feet

carbon 14 dating: radiocarbon (14. C) is a radioactive isotope of carbon, a building block of all life-forms. Because the isotope decays at a constant rate, an organism's death can be dated by calculating the amount of isotope present in its remains.

chelicerae: the first pair of pincerlike appendages on a spider or other arachnid. Its fang-like shape can aid in feeding, or it can inject venom into its prey.

chromatophores: specialized skin cells that allow a creature to change color, texture, or pattern

convergent evolution: when a similar trait evolves in two or more lineages that do not share a common ancestor. For example, the thumb is found in both primates and red pandas, but the skeletal origin of each is different.

crustacean: any of the many invertebrates in the class Crustacea that includes shrimp, lobsters, crabs, and barnacles. Typically water dwelling, they possess hard outer shells and jointed limbs.

cutaneous respiration: an exchange of gases through the skin rather than through an organ such as gills or lungs

cuttlebone: the hard, internal shell of a cuttlefish that is used to maintain buoyancy

deep-sea gigantism: the tendency for creatures in deep-sea regions to grow significantly larger than related species in shallower waters

disruptive coloration: a means of camouflage in which a creature's striking color or pattern breaks up the recognizable shape of its body, thus confusing or escaping a predator's notice

echolocation: a means of navigating or foraging in which a creature emits sounds whose returning echoes—bouncing off objects or potential food sources—are then analyzed and interpreted by its ears and brain

ecosystem: the interconnected community of living things—plants, animals, and microorganisms—that share a specific environment

ectotherm: cold-blooded; a creature that must attain its body temperature from the conditions of its environment

eusocial: a true cooperative social structure within a population, in which there is a distinct reproductive division of labor

folivore: an animal whose diet consists primarily of leaves

fruigivore: an animal whose diet consists primarily of fruits

gular pouch: in birds such as pelicans, an expandable, membrane-like throat that allows the capturing or holding of food

molt: to shed feathers, hair, skin, or an exterior shell as part of an animal's growth or seasonal life cycle

pachyostotic: a solid bone without a spongy inner marrow

parapodia: a bristlelike structure capable of inflicting a sting

phylogenetic relict: the single surviving species in an entire classification

pinna: a mammal's outer ear (plural, pinnae)

primate: excepting humans, these are tree-dwelling mammals characterized by eyes that face forward and both hands and feet that afford the animal agility and dexterity. Primates include humans, monkeys, apes, lemurs, bush babies, tarsiers, and marmosets.

proboscis: a long and particularly flexible nose on a mammal; a tubular mouthpart on an invertebrate such as a butterfly that allows it to feed

skeletal pneumaticity: the honeycomb pockets of air in bones that can become actual air sacs called diverticula

taxonomy: a system of classification. In science a way of identifying, describing, naming, and categorizing organisms to reflect their common ancestry and traits.

tetrapod: an animal with four feet

thermal: a sun-heated column of air that rises. When the sun warms the ground, the air in that lower atmosphere heats up. A thermal is created as that warmer air rises toward the cooler atmosphere. Birds—particularly raptors that sustain longer flights and heavier birds such as vultures and pelicans—depend on that "lift" to conserve energy.

SELECTED BIBLIOGRAPHY

"All about Birds." Cornell Lab of Ornithology. Accessed August 31, 2016. http://www.allaboutbirds.org/guide/search.

Andrei, Mihai. "Why Some Creatures in the Deep Sea Grow to Enormous Sizes." *ZME Science*. Last modified July 8, 2015. http://www.zmescience.com/science/biology/deep-sea-giant-creature.

Animals. *National Geographic*. Accessed August 31, 2016. http://animals.nationalgeographic.com/animals/.

Bug Guide. Iowa State University. Accessed August 31, 2016. http://bugguide.net/node/view/15740.

EDGE. Accessed August 31, 2016. http://www.edgeofexistence.org/index.php.

Fish Index. Accessed August 31, 2016. http://fishindex.blogspot.com/.

Glynn, Ian. *Elegance in Science: The Beauty of Simplicity*. New York: Oxford University Press, 2010.

Gross, Michael. *Life on the Edge: Amazing Creatures Thriving in Extreme Environments*. New York: Perseus, 2001.

Nova Labs. *PBS*. Accessed August 31, 2016. http://www.pbs.org/wgbh/nova/labs/.

Nova Nature. *PBS*. Accessed August 31, 2016. http://www.pbs.org/wgbh/nova/nature/.

Nova Next. *PBS*. Accessed August 31, 2016. http://www.pbs.org/wgbh/nova/next/.

Nova ScienceNow. *PBS*. Accessed August 31, 2016. http://www.pbs.org/wgbh/nova/sciencenow/.

ScienceDaily. Accessed August 31, 2016. https://www.sciencedaily.com/news/plants_animals/.

FURTHER INFORMATION

Books

Blevins, Wiley. *Ninja Plants: Survival and Adaptation in the Plant World*. Minneapolis: Twenty-First Century Books, 2017.
This fascinating and visually appealing book is filled with information about adaptation, evolution, and life cycles within the plant kingdom.

Downer, Ann. *The Animal Mating Game: The Wacky, Weird World of Sex in the Animal Kingdom*. Minneapolis: Twenty-First Century Books, 2017.
This fascinating book highlights some of the unique, dramatic, and interesting techniques animals use to mate and ensure the future of their kind.

———. *Smart and Spineless: Exploring Invertebrate Intelligence*. Minneapolis: Twenty-First Century Books, 2016.
From earthworms to jellyfish, this book takes a look at some of the invertebrates (animals without spines) in the animal kingdom and delves into the question of what it means for animals to be smart.

National Audubon Society Field Guides. New York: Alfred A. Knopf.
This renowned series of field guides created by the National Audubon Society is full of illustrations, diagrams, and accessible text. The series features separate books about birds, amphibians, mammals, and other aspects of the natural world.

Peterson Field Guides. Boston: Houghton Mifflin Harcourt.
This series of field guides by Roger Tory Peterson features illustrations and diagrams along with informative text. The series includes books about fish, reptiles, mollusks, and more.

Simmons, Adam. *Encyclopedia of Adaptations in the Natural World*. Santa Barbara, CA: Greenwood, 2010.

With a novel approach to understanding evolution, the author presents several chapters about the challenges organisms must face. Of added interest is the incorporation of technological breakthroughs that humans have designed based on the natural world.

Trail, Jesse Vernon. *Quiver Trees, Phantom Orchids & Rock Splitters: The Remarkable Survival Strategies of Plants.* Toronto: ECW, 2015.
Focused on the plant kingdom, this volume features species that have evolved to endure conditions that would kill other plants. The book includes chapters on plants' defensive and offensive strategies, as well as solutions to growing, pollinating, and seed dispersal in extreme environments.

Zimmer, Carl. *The Tangled Bank: An Introduction to Evolution.* Greenwood Village, CO: Roberts, 2014.
New York Times award-winning science columnist Carl Zimmer accessibly presents the general concepts of evolution. Originally published in 2009, this 464-page revision includes vividly illustrated chapters on everything from the adaptations of the first land creatures to the evolution of snake venom to the development of new bacteria that can resist antibiotics.

Zimmer, Marc. *Bioluminescence: Nature and Science at Work.* Minneapolis: Twenty-First Century Books, 2015.
Zimmer offers a concise survey of the different ways animals use bioluminescence, the creating of light by means of an enzymatic reaction with the light-emitting compound luciferin.

Films and Videos

Creatures of the Night
http://www.bbc.co.uk/programmes/p00dzfn6
This video clip shows the aye-aye in action at night.

David Attenborough's Natural Curiosities. DVD. London: UKTV, 2013.
In this documentary series, David Attenborough presents incredible evolutionary traits and behaviors found throughout the animal kingdom.

Fish Floats
http://www.bbc.co.uk/programmes/p00f26wj
This video shows how fish float and sink in the water—just like a submarine.

Fishing Fish
http://www.bbc.co.uk/nature/adaptations/Ambush_predator#p006l5bb
Watch this video to learn more about how frogfish disguise themselves and attract prey using their fleshy lures.

Frilled Lizard
http://video.nationalgeographic.com/video/lizard_frilled_ontherun
Check out this video to see a frilled lizard's outrageous adaptations in action.

Frozen Planet. DVD. London: BBC Home Entertainment, 2011.
This documentary series focuses on life in the Arctic and Antarctica—the two least hospitable places on the planet. The harsh life of polar bears, seals, and penguins is featured, as well as that of two human communities in the far north of Siberia and Finland.

Life. DVD. Bristol, UK: BBC, 2010.
Produced by the BBC and the Discovery Channel, this eleven-part, landmark series on natural history is narrated by Oprah Winfrey and features 130 diverse stories of the plants and animals occupying every sort of ecological niche.

Mudskippers
http://video.nationalgeographic.com/video/mudskippers
This video shows the mudskipper in action, living life on land.

Planet Earth II. DVD. London: BBC Home Entertainment, 2017.
These episodes take a look at Earth from the viewpoint of the planet's animals. New recording techniques have improved clarity, detail, and drama. From jungles to islands, cities to deserts, the world's wildlife offers an unprecedented look at the planet we share.

World's Weirdest: Proboscis Monkeys
  http://video.nationalgeographic.com/video/weirdest-proboscis
  -monkey
  Watch this video to learn more about how the proboscis monkey
  uses its large nose.

Websites

Animal Diversity Web
  http://animaldiversity.ummz.umich.edu/site/index.html
  Hosted by the University of Michigan Museum of Zoology, this
  searchable database profiles the natural history of thousands of
  animal species in a searchable, encyclopedic format.

Arkive
  http://www.arkive.org/
  Sponsored by the nonprofit group Wildscreen, this site engages
  remarkable filmmakers and photographers to curate an ever-
  expanding showcase of the planet's creatures. Each is featured
  in a slide show with discussions of habitat, conservation status,
  biology, range, and classification, as well as links to further
  resources.

Encyclopedia of Life
  http://www.eol.org/
  This comprehensive gathering of data, photos, videos, and links
  from journals, scientific collections, books, and online resources
  showcases all forms of life from mushrooms to marsupials,
  protozoans to primates, algae to arachnids.

42Evolution
  http://www.42evolution.org
  An online magazine of readable and fascinating articles, this site
  includes profiles of pioneers in the field, a question-and-answer
  section, and a wealth of videos, graphics, games, and links. This
  truly engaging resource is the brainchild of a preeminent team
  of contributing scientists from several disciplines.

IUCN Red List of Threatened Species
  http://www.iucnredlist.org/
  The International Union for the Conservation of Nature and

Natural Resources (IUCN) has maintained the most widely used global reference on the conservation status of every animal and plant. The site also includes a bibliography, photo album, and discussion of each creature.

MarineBio
http://marinebio.org/search/
This conservation site, headed by a network of experts, features substantive articles about marine ecology, global warming, aquatic biodiversity, alien species, sustainable ecotourism, habitat destruction, and more.

PHOTO ACKNOWLEDGMENTS

The images in this book are used with the permission of: Hemis/Alamy Stock Photo, p. 4; iStock.com/stockcam, p. 6; © Michael Durham/Minden Pictures, p. 8; © Laura Westlund/Independent Picture Service, pp. 10, 11, 23, 28, 66; Frans Lanting StudioAlamy Stock Photo, p. 12; © Pete Oxford/Minden Pictures, p. 14; iStock.com/CathyKeifer, p. 15; © Fabio Liverani/ npl/Minden Pictures, p. 18; © Remi Masson/Minden Pictures, p. 20; John Cancalosi/Alamy Stock Photo, p. 22; Doug Wilson/Alamy Stock Photo, p. 26; Genevieve Vallee/Alamy Stock Photo, p. 29; © Georgette Douwma/NPL/Minden Pictures, p. 31; Douglas Faulkner/Photo Researchers RM/Getty Images, p. 33; iStock.com/prasit_chansareekorn, p. 36; dpa picture alliance archive/Alamy Stock Photo, p. 39; Steve Downeranth/Pantheon/Superstock, p. 42; Stocktrek Images, Inc./Alamy Stock Photo, p. 45; WaterFrame/Alamy Stock Photo, p. 47; Tammy Wolfe/Alamy Stock Photo, p. 48; blickwinkel/Alamy Stock Photo, p. 50; Ross Armstrong/Alamy Stock Photo, p. 51; © Jurgen Freund/Minden Pictures, p. 53; Nature Picture Library/Alamy Stock Photo, p. 54; Rafael Ben-Ari/Alamy Stock Photo, p. 59; © Neil Aldridge/Minden Pictures, p. 60; © Lou Coetzer/Minden Pictures, p. 62; Uwe Bergwitz/Shutterstock.com, p. 63; Greg Brave/Shutterstock.com, p. 65; © Laura Westlund/Independent Picture Service, p. 66; Bruce Miller/Alamy Stock Photo, p. 67; iStock.com/cowboy5437, p. 69; Frans Lanting Studio/Alamy Stock Photo, p. 70; Michael Freeman/Alamy Stock Photo, p. 73; robertharding/Alamy Stock Photo, p. 76; Bildagentur Zoonar GmbH/Shutterstock.com, p. 79; © Jan-Luc van Eijk/Minden Pictures, p. 81; RooM the Agency/Alamy Stock Photo, p. 82; iStock.com/dangdumrong, p. 87.

Front cover: Stephen Dalton/ Minden Picturesy/Getty Images.

INDEX

ABOUT THE AUTHOR

Michael J. Rosen is the author, editor, illustrator, or photographer of more than 135 books for both adults and children. They range from short-story collections to poetry, from cookbooks to humor anthologies, and from picture books to teen nonfiction. Among recent books are *A Tale of Rescue*, a novel chosen as one of *Kirkus Reviews* and the New York Public Library's best books of the year; a full-length play based on his National Jewish Book Award-winning picture book, *Elijah's Angel*; and three volumes of haiku about cats, dogs, and birds, which received a trifecta of stars from *Kirkus Reviews*. Rosen's nonfiction titles for teens include *Just My Type: Understanding Personality Profiles*, *Place Hacking: Venturing Off Limits*, and *Girls vs. Guys: Surprising Differences between the Sexes*.

Many of Rosen's books engage his degree in zoology and his passion for nature and the creatures that share this world. For more than two decades, he's shared one hundred forested acres in the foothills of the Appalachians, east of Columbus, Ohio. His website is www.michaeljrosen.com.